irresistible knits

CREDITS

President, Nancy J. Martin
CEO, Daniel J. Martin
Publisher, Jane Hamada
Editorial Director, Mary V. Green
Editorial Project Manager, Tina Cook
Technical Editor, Jane Townswick
Copy Editor, Liz McGehee
Design and Production Manager, Stan Green
Cover and Text Designer, Renata Chubb, Mighty Integrated Inc.
Photographer, John Scully, Big Red Photography
Art Direction and Styling, Kirsten Cowan

Irresistible Knits: Sweaters for Men, Women, and Teens
© 2001 by Kirsten Cowan

Martingale & Company
20205 144th Ave. NE
Woodinville, WA 98072
www.martingale-pub.com

Martingale™
& C O M P A N Y

Kirsten Cowan
NEEDLEWORKS

Printed in China
06 05 04 03 02 01   6 5 4 3 2 1

Library of Congress Cataloging-in-Publication Data is available
ISBN: 1-56477-372-8

MISSION STATEMENT

We are dedicated to providing quality products and service by working together to inspire creativity and to enrich the lives we touch.

irresistible knits

SWEATERS FOR MEN, WOMEN, AND TEENS

Kirsten Cowan

Martingale™
& COMPANY

This book is dedicated to Craig and Elizabeth,
with more love than I can say.

acknowledgments

I wish to thank John Scully, whose photography brings these designs to light,
Mary Green and Jane Townswick, whose editing brings the book to fruition, and Renata Chubb
at Mighty Integrated Inc., whose design brings it all together.

My knitters – April, Bev, Diane, Dollé, Grace, Maud, Pat, and Terry – worked cheerfully
under tight deadlines. The Hodder family provided a wonderful location and canine model, Molly.

Thanks also to the yarn companies whose yarns are featured in this book, most especially to
Gayle, Sara, Dino, and Josie for your support.

Finally, my thanks to my family for their encouragement.

table of contents

autumn

winter

spring

introduction

During the making of this book, I inherited a knitting caddy – stocked with wooden needles, the thinnest of crochet hooks, and elaborate Bakelite-handled scissors – that had belonged to my great-grandmother. She was of a generation of women who possessed knitting as an obligatory skill, along with cooking, cleaning, and caring for children.

Times do change, and now women and men knit for the sheer pleasure of it, often as an antidote to our modern-day obligations, to create a self-contained oasis of calm. We enjoy creating unique sweaters for ourselves and for the people we love – our partners, our children.

This book was conceived for knitters who are looking for patterns both in adult sizes and sizes for teenagers. Traditionally, knitting patterns come either in children's sizes (up to size 10) or in adult sizes, leaving a gap in between. I've addressed the need for those in-between sizes: kids from the age of 12 to 16 who are too big for children's sweaters yet too small for adults' sweaters.

While many of the patterns in this book incorporate both adult and teen sizes, these options take different design tacks. The sweaters modeled by teen girls, for example, tend to be cropped or closer to the body, and feature bright, funky colors. In the designs for women and men, on the other hand, I've tried to stick to an approach that one of my readers says "pushes traditional to exquisite."

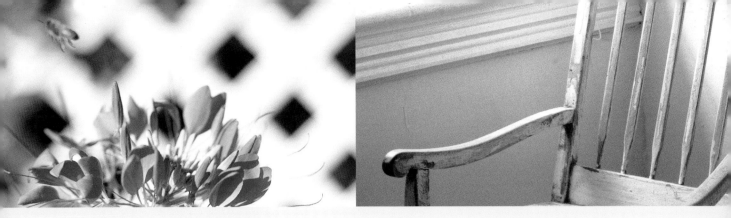

"Many a garden," as the French author Colette said, "has left its memory with me," and many a quilt, a vintage sweater, a stonework crest, a glimpse through leaves – all of these inspirations have soaked in and somehow emerged as drawings in my sketchbooks. Fashion, too, permeates most aspects of our lives whether we're aware of it or not, and my aim is to design knits that are stylish and modern, yet timeless.

There's never been a better time for creative, inspiring, unique knitting: references to knitting in the media, the plethora of gorgeous yarns now available, and the importance of knits on fashion runways have all transpired to pique the interest of more and more people in hand knitting. For teens who are interested in learning to knit, I hope the designs in this book provide inspiration – many of the patterns are ideal for novice knitters. At the back of the book, you'll find lots of useful tips and diagrams to get you started.

When I pick up the needles that my great-grandmother and, after her, my grandmother used, it's a way of remembering them. And by designing for today's knitters, I participate in making an ancient craft part of the present – I hope you enjoy taking part, too.

KIRSTEN COWAN

autumn

autumn

Leaves have long been a recurring motif in my work. In this generously scaled shawl-collared cardigan, leaves of oak, maple, and birch drift over patches worked in autumnal heather yarns. (The knitter who made this sweater for me thought it would be beautiful without the leaves, too!)

SKILL LEVEL: INTERMEDIATE/EXPERIENCED

MEASUREMENTS

SIZES (in inches)		WOMEN		
	SM	MD	LG	XL
Finished Chest	45	46½	49	50½
Finished Length	30	30	30	30

MATERIALS

Yarn: MC, A – Naturally Guernsey Aran 10 Ply 100% Wool (181 yds or 167 m/100 gr ball). B, C, D, E – Patons Classic Merino 100% Wool (221 yds or 204 m/100 gr ball). *See also page 126 for yarn information.*

NO. OF BALLS		WOMEN		
	SM	MD	LG	XL
MC: Burgundy #214	6	6	7	7
A: Chestnut #216	4	4	5	5
B: Loden #205	3	3	4	4
C: Paprika #238	1	1	1	1
D: Old Gold #204	1	1	1	1
E: Purple #212	1	1	1	1

Needles: 1 pr. U.S. size 7 (4.5 mm) needles OR SIZE TO OBTAIN GAUGE

U.S. size 7 (4.5 mm) 24" or 29" (45 cm or 60 cm) circular needle for collar

Five 1¼" buttons

GAUGE

20 sts and 26 rows = 4" in st st

To work Gauge Swatch: with MC, cast on 24 sts and work st st (k all sts on RS and p all sts on WS). Work until piece measures 5" from bottom edge. Bind off. Block swatch by laying flat and applying lots of steam with steam iron held just above the swatch. Let cool and dry. If you have too many sts and rows to the inch, switch to a larger needle; too few means you should use a smaller needle.

Your garment will not fit properly if the tension gauge is incorrect! Take the time to check by making gauge swatch.

Directions are given for size Small. Sizes Medium, Large, and Extra-Large are given in parentheses. Where there is only one number, it applies to all sizes.

BACK

With MC, cast on 111 (111, 117, 123) sts. Work ribbing as follows:

RS rows: p3, *k3, p3*, rep from * to end.

WS rows: k3, *p3, k3*, rep from * to end.

Rep the last 2 rows 5 more times and inc 1 (5, 5, 3) sts evenly across last row. You should now have 112 (116, 122, 126) sts.

Begin working Back chart, working armhole and shoulder shaping as indicated until chart is complete. Work each color area with separate ball of yarn in intarsia method; you can also use duplicate stitch for smaller details. (See page 123 for more information on intarsia knitting, and page 124 for duplicate st.) Bind off.

RIGHT AND LEFT FRONTS

With MC, cast on 45 (51, 51, 57) sts. Work ribbing as follows:

RS rows: k3, *p3, k3*, rep from * to end.

Lower Half of Front and Back Chart

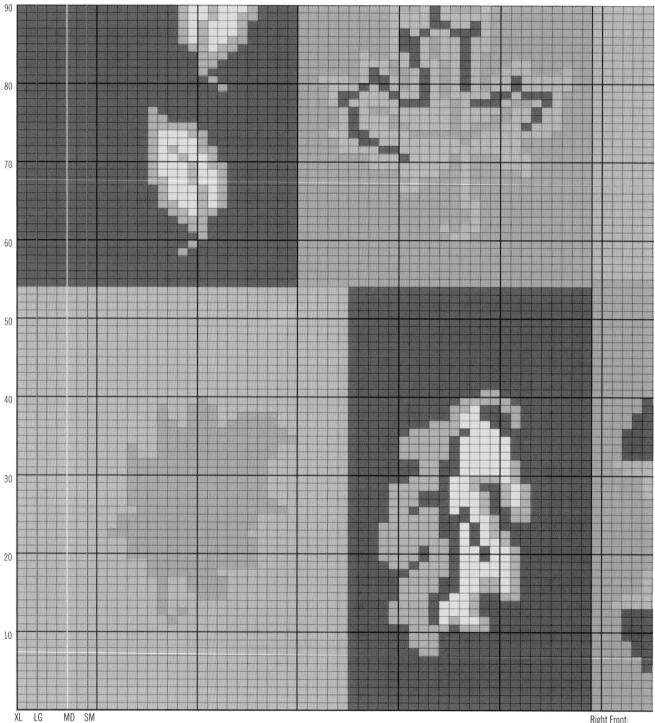

Right Front:
Begin RS rows here

Legend:
- MC
- A
- B
- C
- D
- E

XL LG MD SM

Lower Half of Front and Back Chart

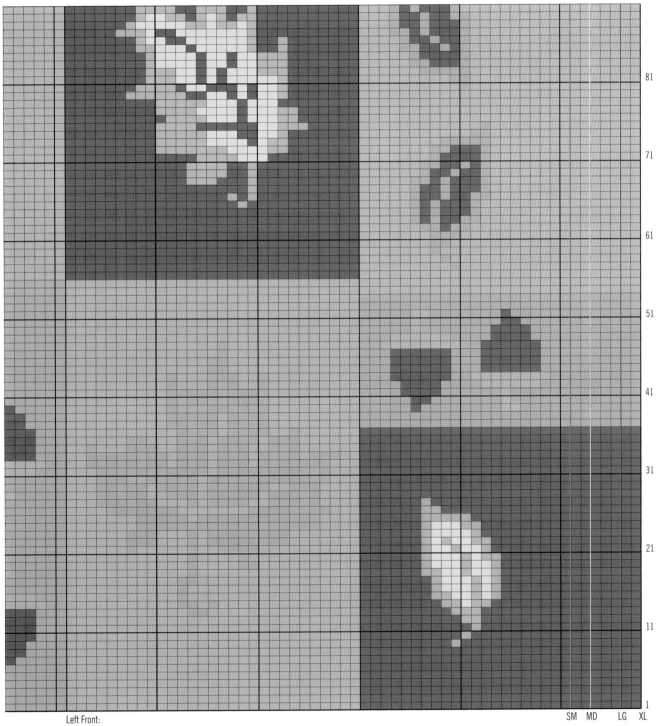

81

71

61

51

41

31

21

11

1

Left Front:
End RS rows here

SM   MD   LG   XL

MC
A
B
C
D
E

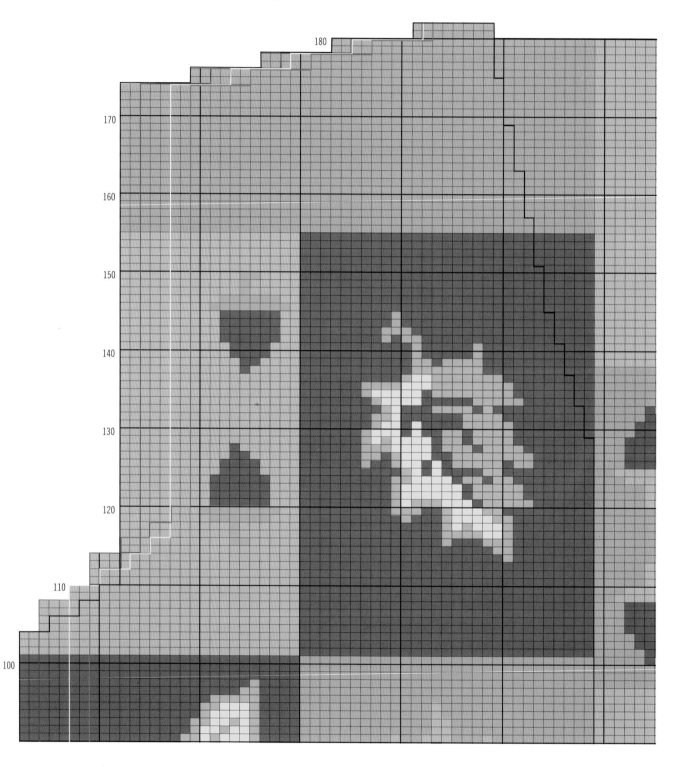

Upper Half of Front and Back Chart

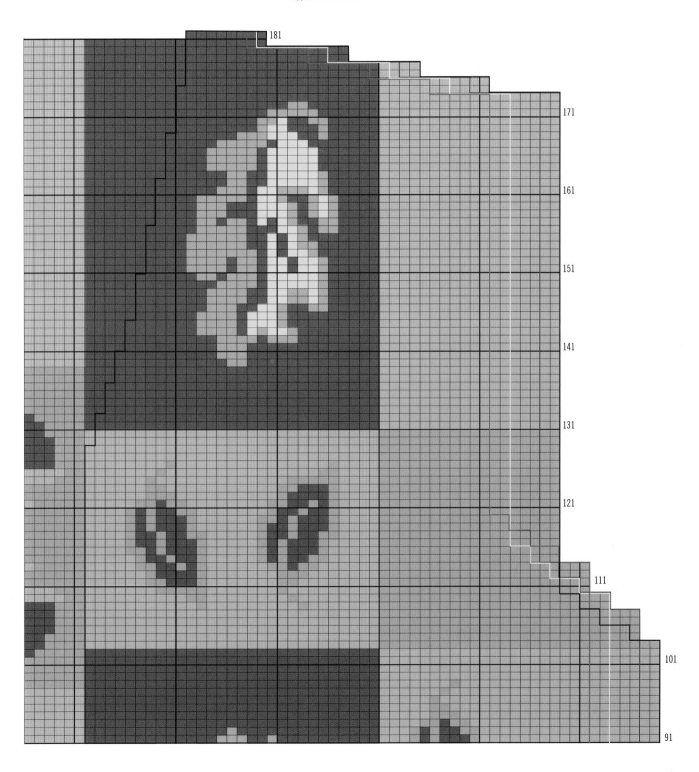

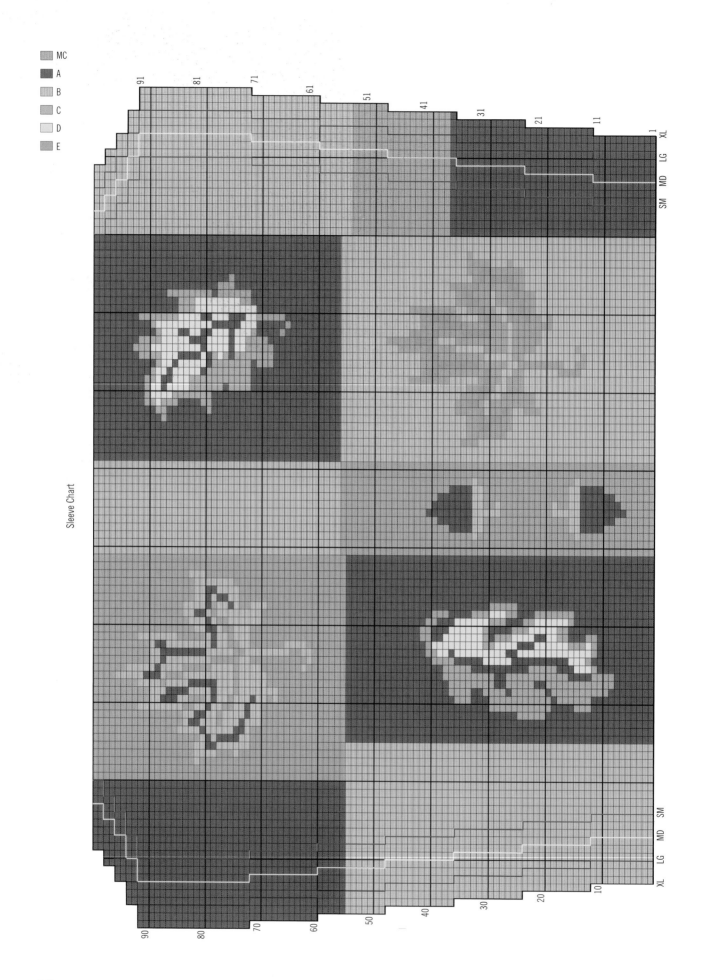

Sleeve Chart

MC
A
B
C
D
E

WS rows: p3, *k3, p3*, rep from * to end.

Rep the last 2 rows 5 more times and inc 5 (1, 4, 0) sts, evenly across last row. You should now have 50 (52, 55, 57) sts.

Work Right Front or Left Front chart, working neck shaping and armhole shaping as indicated.

SLEEVES

With MC, cast on 78 (84, 90, 96) sts.

Work [k3, p3] ribbing until piece measures 5½ (6, 6, 6½") from bottom edge, ending with RS facing for next row.

Begin working sleeve chart, making incs and bind offs at sides as indicated until chart is complete. Bind off.

FINISHING

Sew shoulder seams.

Note: Collar is worked in 2 sections, with a seam at center back.

Right Collar: with MC, cast on 182 sts and work ribbing as follows:

RS rows: k2, *p3, k3* rep from * to end.

WS rows: *p3, k3* rep to last 2 sts, p2.

Rep the last 2 rows 3 times more, then work one more RS row.

Next row (WS): keeping in rib pat as established, work 5 buttonholes as follows: work 3 sts, *bind off 2 sts, work 21 sts*, rep 3 more times, bind off 2 sts, work rib pat to end.

Next row (RS): work rib pat; when you come to bound-off sts for buttonholes, turn and cast on 2 sts, turn again and resume working rib. Work 6 more rows in rib as established.

Begin shaping (WS): bind off 104 sts in pat, work in rib to end. Continue working rib, binding off sts at beginning of WS rows in the following sequence: bind off 2 sts 10 times, bind off 3 sts four times, bind off 4 sts twice. On next WS row, bind off remaining sts.

Left Collar: with MC, cast on 182 sts and work ribbing as follows:

RS rows: *k3, p3*, rep to last 2 sts, k2.

WS rows: p2, *k3, p3*, rep from * to end.

Work remainder of collar as mirror image of Right Collar, omitting buttonholes and working shaping by binding off at beginning of RS rows.

Sew center back collar seam. Whipstitch collar to Front edges, placing curved edge of collar at Front edges and placing collar seam at center back neck. Sew side seams. Sew sleeve seams and upper half of cuff seams. With WS together, sew lower half of cuff seams, thus reversing seam for fold-back. Set in sleeves. Sew buttons to correspond to buttonholes.

QUICK TIP: *When changing colors at the beginning of a row, wind the tail ends around the working yarn on the wrong side for the first five or six stitches — it's faster than darning the ends in later.*

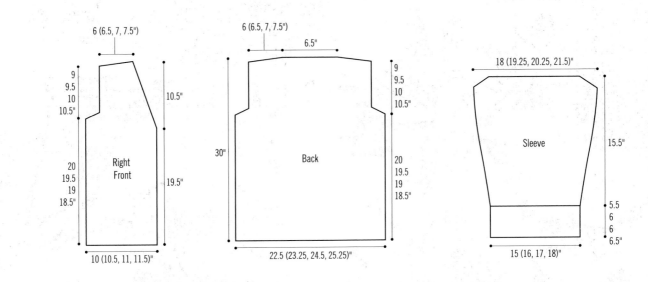

Right Front
6 (6.5, 7, 7.5")
9
9.5
10
10.5"
10.5"
20
19.5
19
18.5"
19.5"
10 (10.5, 11, 11.5)"

Back
6 (6.5, 7, 7.5")
6.5"
9
9.5
10
10.5"
30"
20
19.5
19
18.5"
22.5 (23.25, 24.5, 25.25)"

Sleeve
18 (19.25, 20.25, 21.5)"
15.5"
5.5
6
6
6.5"
15 (16, 17, 18)"

melrose

Sometimes my favorite designs come about as a response to a challenge – in this case, to design a man's sweater that looks unique and fresh, yet uses only knit and purl stitches. I was especially happy with the curved mock seams, worked with simple increases and decreases, and the way the three different textured patterns interact. Both charts and written instructions are given for this design.

SKILL LEVEL: INTERMEDIATE

MEASUREMENTS

SIZES (in inches)	ADULTS			
	SM	MD	LG	XL
Finished Chest	46	48	54	55½
Finished Length	25	25	27¾	27¾

MATERIALS

Yarn: Butterfly Super 10 100% Cotton #3307 (249 yds or 230 m/125 gr skein). *See also page 126 for yarn information.*

NO. OF SKEINS	ADULTS			
	SM	MD	LG	XL
Cotton #3307	5	5	6	7

Needles: 1 pr. each U.S. sizes 6 and 7 (4 mm and 4.5 mm) needles OR SIZE TO OBTAIN GAUGE

Spare needle or stitch holder

GAUGE

20 sts and 30 rows = 4" in st st using larger needles

To work Gauge Swatch: with larger needles, cast on 24 sts and work st st (k all sts on RS and p all sts on WS) until piece measures 5" from bottom edge. Bind off. Block swatch by laying flat and applying lots of steam with steam iron held just above the swatch. Let cool and dry. If you have too many sts and rows to the inch, switch to a larger needle; too few means you should use a smaller needle.

Your garment will not fit properly if the tension gauge is incorrect! Take the time to check by making gauge swatch.

Directions are given for size Small. Sizes Medium, Large, and Extra-Large are given in parentheses. Where there is only one number, it applies to all sizes.

LOWER FRONT

With smaller needles, cast on 114 (120, 132, 138) sts.

Beginning with a WS row, work 3 rows garter st (k all sts on all rows).

Begin diagonal pat, working from Chart I on page 23 or written directions as follows:

Row 1 (RS): *p2, k3, p1*, rep from * to end.

Row 2 (WS): *k2, p3, k1*, rep from * to end.

Row 3 (RS): *k3, p3*, rep from * to end.

Row 4 (WS): *p1, k3, p2*, rep from * to end.

Row 5 (RS): *k1, p3, k2*, rep from * to end.

Row 6 (WS): *p3, k3*, rep from * to end.

Row 7 (RS): *p2, k3, p1*, rep from * to end.

Row 8 (WS): *k2, p3, k1*, rep from * to end.

Row 9 (RS): *k3, p3*, rep from * to end.

Work 2 rows garter st.

Next row (WS): k and inc 1 (1, 2, 0) st(s) evenly across row to 115 (121, 134, 138) sts.

Change to larger needles and begin main body pattern, working either from charted or written instructions as indicated.

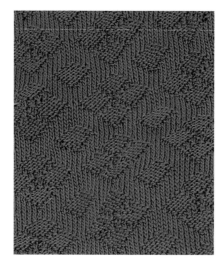

CHARTED INSTRUCTIONS

Place charts as follows, reading RS rows on chart from right to left, and WS rows from left to right:

Row 1 (RS): k2 (5, 3, 5), work Row 1 of Chart II twice, [p2, k1] twice, work Row 1 of Chart III 3 (3, 4, 4) times, [k1, p2] twice, work Row 1 of Chart IV twice, k2 (5, 3, 5).

Row 2 (WS): p2 (5, 3, 5), work Row 2 of Chart IV twice, [k2, p1] twice, work Row 2 of Chart III 3 (3, 4, 4) times, [p1, k2] twice, work Row 2 of Chart II twice, p2 (5, 3, 5).

Charted pats are now in position; continue working to end of charts, repeating 10 rows of Charts II and IV twice for every 20 rows of Chart III.

Skip to "Armhole Shaping."

WRITTEN INSTRUCTIONS

Row 1 (RS): k2 (5, 3, 5), *p3, k3*, rep from * 3 more times, [p2, k1] twice, *p4, k9, p4*, rep from * 2 (2, 3, 3) more times, [k1, p2] twice, *k3, p3*, rep from * 3 more times, k2 (5, 3, 5).

Row 2 (WS): p2 (5, 3, 5), *[p1, k3] twice, p4*, rep from * once more, [k2, p1] twice, *k3, p11, k3*, rep from * 2 (2, 3, 3) more times, [p1, k2] twice, *p4, [k3, p1] twice*, rep from * once more, p2 (5, 3, 5).

Row 3 (RS): k2 (5, 3, 5), *k2, p5, k5*, rep from * once more, [p2, k1] twice, *p2, k6, p1, k6, p2*, rep from * 2 (2, 3, 3) more times, [k1, p2] twice, *k5, p5, k2*, rep from * once more, k2 (5, 3, 5).

Row 4 (WS): p2 (5, 3, 5), *p3, k3, p6*, rep from * once more, [k2, p1] twice, *k1, p6, k3, p6, k1*, rep from * 2 (2, 3, 3) more times, [p1, k2] twice, *p6, k3, p3*, rep from * once more, p2 (5, 3, 5).

Row 5 (RS): k2 (5, 3, 5), *k4, p1, k7*, rep from * once more, [p2, k1] twice, *k6, p5, k6*, rep from * 2 (2, 3, 3) more times, [k1, p2] twice, *k7, p1, k4*, rep from * once more, k2 (5, 3, 5).

Row 6 (WS): p26 (29, 27, 29), [k2, p1] twice, *p5, k7, p5*, rep from * 2 (2, 3, 3) more times, [p1, k2] twice, p to end.

Row 7 (RS): Rep Row 5.

Row 8 (WS): p2 (5, 3, 5), *p3, k3, p6*, rep from * once more, [k2, p1] twice, *p4, k1, p2, k3, p2, k1, p4*, rep from * 2 (2, 3, 3) more times, [p1, k2] twice, *p6, k3, p3*, rep from * once more, p2 (5, 3, 5).

Row 9 (RS): k2 (5, 3, 5), *k2, p5, k5*, rep from * once more, [p2, k1] twice, *k3, p3, k2, p1, k2, p3, k3*, rep from * 2 (2, 3, 3) more times, [k1, p2] twice, *k5, p5, k2*, rep from * once more, k2 (5, 3, 5).

Row 10 (WS): p2 (5, 3, 5), *[p1, k3] twice, p4*, rep from * once more, [k2, p1] twice, *p2, k5, p1, k1, p1, k5, p2*, rep from * 2 (2, 3, 3) more times, [p1, k2], *p4, [k3, p1] twice*, rep from * once more, p2 (5, 3, 5).

Row 11 (RS): k2 (5, 3, 5), *p3, k3*, rep from * 3 more times, [p2, k1] twice, *[k1, p7] twice, k1*, rep from * 2 (2, 3, 3) more times, [k1, p2] twice, *k3, p3*, rep from * 3 more times, k2 (5, 3, 5).

Row 12 (WS): rep Row 10.

Row 13 (RS): rep Row 9.

Row 14 (WS): rep Row 8.

Row 15 (RS): rep Row 7.

Row 16 (WS): rep Row 6.

Row 17 (RS): rep Row 5.

Row 18 (WS): rep Row 4.

Row 19 (RS): rep Row 3.

Row 20 (WS): rep Row 2.

Armhole shaping: Repeat last 20 rows 4 (4, 5, 5) more times, then work Rows 1 and 2 once more. AT THE SAME TIME, when piece measures 15½ (15, 17¼, 17¼)" from bottom edge, work armhole shaping as follows: bind off first 14 (17, 15, 17) sts on each of the next 2 rows and work in pat to end. You should now have 87 (87, 104, 104) sts remaining.

Begin mock seam shaping (beginning

with Row 3 of pat, and noting that Chart III pat is still worked between *....*):

Row 3 (RS): k2, p5, k3, k2tog, p2, k1, p2, inc 1, *p2, k6, p1, k6, p2*, rep from * 2 (2, 3, 3) more times, inc 1, p2, k1, p2, sl 1, k1, psso, k3, p5, k2.

Row 4 (WS): p3, k3, p5, k2, p1, k2, p2, *k1, p6, k3, p6, k1*, rep from * 2 (2, 3, 3) more times, p2, k2, p1, k2, p5, k3, p3.

Row 5 (RS): k4, p1, k4, k2tog, p2, k1, p2, inc 1, k1, *k6, p5, k6*, rep from * 2 (2, 3, 3) more times, k1, inc 1, p2, k1, p2, sl 1, k1, psso, k4, p1, k4.

Row 6 (WS): p10, k2, p1, k2, p3, *p5, k7, p5*, rep from * 2 (2, 3, 3) more times, p3, k2, p1, k2, p10.

Row 7 (RS): k8, k2tog, p2, k1, p2, inc 1, k2, *k6, p5, k6*, rep from * 2 (2, 3, 3) more times, k2, inc 1, p2, k1, p2, sl 1, k1, psso, k8.

Row 8 (WS): p9, k2, p1, k2, p4, *p4, k1, p2, k3, p2, k1, p4*, rep from * 2 (2, 3, 3) more times, p4, k2, p1, k2, p9.

Row 9 (RS): k7, k2tog, p2, k1, p2, inc 1, k3, *k3, p3, k2, p1, k2, p3, k3*, rep from * 2 (2, 3, 3) more times, k3, inc 1, p2, k1, p2, sl 1, k1, psso, k7.

Row 10 (WS): p8, k2, p1, k2, p5, *p2, k5, p1, k1, p1, k5, p2*, rep from * 2 (2, 3, 3) more times, p5, k2, p1, k2, p8.

Row 11 (RS): k6, k2tog, p2, k1, p2, inc 1, k4, *[k1, p7] twice, k1*, rep from * 2 (2, 3, 3) more times, k4, inc 1, p2, k1, p2, sl 1, k1, psso, k6.

Row 12 (WS): p7, k2, p1, k2, p6, *p2, k5, p1, k1, p1, k5, p2*, rep from * 2 (2, 3, 3) more times, p6, k2, p1, k2, p7.

Row 13 (RS): k5, k2tog, p2, k1, p2, inc 1, k5, *k3, p3, k2, p1, k2, p3, k3*, rep from * 2 (2, 3, 3) more times, k5, inc 1, p2, k1, p2, sl 1, k1, psso, k5.

Row 14 (WS): p6, k2, p1, k2, p7, *p4, k1, p2, k3, p2, k1, p4*, rep from * 2 (2, 3, 3) more times, p7, k2, p1, k2, p6.

Row 15 (RS): k4, k2tog, p2, k1, p2, inc 1, k6, *k6, p5, k6*, rep from * 2 (2, 3, 3) more times, k6, inc 1, p2, k1, p2, sl 1, k1, psso, k4.

Row 16 (WS): p5, k2, p1, k2, p8, *p5, k7, p5*, rep from * 2 (2, 3, 3) more times, p8, k2, p1, k2, p5.

Row 17 (RS): k3, k2tog, p2, k1, p2, inc 1, k7, *k6, p5, k6*, rep from * 2 (2, 3, 3) more times, k7, inc 1, p2, k1, p2, sl 1, k1, psso, k3

Row 18 (WS): p2, p2tog, k2, p1, k2, inc 1 purlwise, p7, k1, *k1, p6, k3, p6, k1*, rep from * 2 (2, 3, 3) more times, k1, p7, inc 1 purlwise, k2, p1, k2, p2tog, p2.

Row 19 (RS): k1, k2tog, p2, k1, p2, inc 1, k7, p2, *p2, k6, p1, k6, p2*, rep from * 2 (2, 3, 3) more times, p2, k7, inc 1, p2, k1, p2, sl 1, k1, psso, k1.

Row 20 (WS): p2tog, k2, p1, k2, inc 1 purlwise, p7, k3, *k3, p11, k3*, rep from * 2 (2, 3, 3) more times, k3, p7, inc 1 purlwise, k2, p1, k2, p2tog.

Row 21 (RS): k2tog, p1, k1, p2, inc 1, k7, p4, *p4, k9, p4*, rep from * 2 (2, 3, 3) more times, p4, k7, inc 1, p2, k1, p1, k2tog.

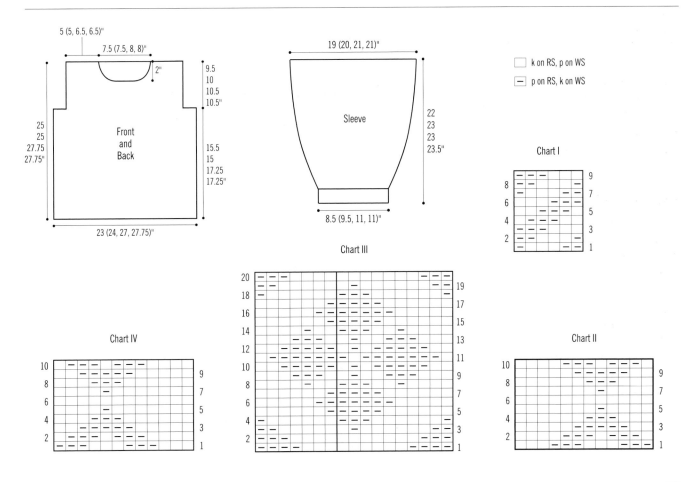

5 (5, 6.5, 6.5)"
7.5 (7.5, 8, 8)"
2"
9.5
10
10.5
10.5"
25
25
27.75
27.75"
Front and Back
15.5
15
17.25
17.25"
23 (24, 27, 27.75)"

19 (20, 21, 21)"
Sleeve
22
23
23
23.5"
8.5 (9.5, 11, 11)"

☐ k on RS, p on WS
– p on RS, k on WS

Chart I
Chart III
Chart IV
Chart II

SHOULDER AND NECK

Continue through rows of chart or written pat as established until piece measures as close as possible to 7½ (8, 8½, 8½)" above armhole shaping, ending with Row 10 or Row 20 of pat.

Work 2 rows garter st.

Left neck shaping (RS): k38 (38, 46, 46). Turn. Put remaining sts for right neck on stitch holder.

Next row (WS): bind off 4 (4, 5, 5) sts, k to end of row.

Next row (RS): begin diagonal pat as given for Front hem band (Chart I) and work to last 2 sts, k2tog.

Next row (WS): bind off 2 sts, work in pat to end.

Next row (RS): work in pat to last 2 sts, k2tog.

Rep last 2 rows once more.

Continue in pat, binding off 1 st at beginning of WS rows until you have 25 (25, 32, 32) sts remaining.

When 9 rows of diagonal pat in Chart I are complete, work 3 rows garter st. Bind off remaining sts.

Right neck shaping: with RS facing, tie on yarn and bind off 11 (11, 12, 12) sts, then k to end.

Next row (WS): k to last 2 sts, k2tog.

Next row (RS): bind off 4 (4, 5, 5) sts, then work diagonal pat as given for Front hem band (Chart I) to end.

Next row (WS): work in pat to last 2 sts, k2tog.

Next row (RS): bind off 2 sts, work in pat to end.

Rep last 2 rows once more.

Continue in pat, binding off 1 st at beginning of RS rows until you have 25 (25, 32, 32) sts remaining.

When 9 rows of diagonal pat are complete, work 3 rows garter st.

Bind off remaining sts.

Row 22 (WS): k2tog, p1, k2, inc 1 purlwise, p9, k3, *k3, p11, k3*, rep from * 2 (2, 3, 3) more times, k3, p9, inc 1 purlwise, k2, p1, k2tog.

Row 23 (RS): k2tog, p2, inc 1, k4, p1, k6, p2, *p2, k6, p1, k6, p2*, rep from * 2 (2, 3, 3) more times, p2, k6, p1, k4, inc 1, p2, k2tog.

Row 24 (WS): k2tog, k1, inc 1 purlwise, p4, k3, p6, k1, *k1, p6, k3, p6, k1*, rep from * 2 (2, 3, 3) more times, k1, p6, k3, p4, inc 1 purlwise, k1, k2tog.

UPPER FRONT

Work upper front from either charted instructions or written instructions as follows:

CHARTED INSTRUCTIONS

Hereafter, work Chart III motif across all sts, with placement as follows:

Next row (RS): k1, *work Row 5 of Chart III*, rep from * 4 (4, 5, 5) more times, k1.

Next row (WS): p1, *work Row 6 of Chart III*, rep from * 4 (4, 5, 5) more times, p1.

Chart is now in position. Skip to "Shoulder and Neck."

WRITTEN INSTRUCTIONS

Hereafter, work central motif across all sts, with placement as follows:

Next row (RS): k1, *follow Row 5 directions between asterisks as given on page 23*, rep from * 4 (4, 5, 5) more times, k1.

Next row (WS): p1, *follow Row 6 directions between asterisks as given on page 23*, rep from * 4 (4, 5, 5) more times, p1.

Continue in this manner, working directions between asterisks as indicated above and working first and last st in st st.

BACK

Work as for Front to "Left neck shaping."

Next row (RS): k and dec 3 (3, 2, 2) sts evenly across row. You should now have 84 (84, 102, 102) sts.

Work 9 rows diagonal pat (Chart I) as given for Front.

Work 3 rows garter st. Bind off all sts knitwise.

SLEEVES

With smaller needles, cast on 42 (48, 54, 54) sts.

Beginning with a WS row, work 3 rows garter st.

Work 9 rows diagonal pat as given for Front.

Work 3 rows garter st and inc 1 (7, 1, 1) st(s) at center of row to 43 (55, 55, 55) sts.

Note: read through remaining directions before proceeding.

Change to larger needles and work pat as follows:

Row 1 (RS): k2, place marker on needle before next st, *k3, p3*, rep from * to last 5 sts, place marker on needle before next st, k5. (Hereafter, work Chart IV between markers.)

Row 2 (WS): p to marker, *[p1, k3] twice, p4*, rep from * to marker, p to end.

Row 3 (RS): k to marker, *k5, p5, k2*, rep from * to marker, k to end.

Row 4 (WS): p to marker, *p3, k3, p6*, rep from * to marker, p to end.

Row 5 (RS): inc 1, k to marker, *k7, p1, k4*, rep from * to marker, k to last st, inc 1.

Row 6 (WS): purl.

Row 7 (RS): k to marker, *k7, p1, k4*, rep from * to marker, k to end.

Row 8 (WS): rep Row 4.

Row 9 (RS): inc 1, k to marker, *k5, p5, k2*, rep from * to marker, k to last st, inc 1.

Row 10 (WS): rep Row 2.

Row 11 (RS): k to marker, *[k3, p3] twice*, rep from * to marker, k to end.

Rep last 10 rows to form pat, and continue working incs at each side every 4th row. Work your incs in st st until you have increased a full pat repeat of 12 sts at each side, then work pat across full row.

When you have 95 (101, 107, 107) sts, work even until piece measures as close as possible to 20 (21, 21, 21½)" from bottom edge, ending with Row 6 or Row 10 of pat.

Work 2 rows garter st, and inc 1 st at center of last row to 96 (102, 108, 108) sts.

Work 9 rows diagonal pat (Chart I) as given for Front. Work 3 rows garter st.

Bind off knitwise.

FINISHING

Sew right shoulder seam.

Collar: with RS facing and larger needles, pick up and knit 25 (25, 26, 26) sts along left Front neck edge, 25 (25, 26, 26) sts along right Front neck edge, and 34 (34, 38, 38) sts along Back neck edge for a total of 84 (84, 90, 90) sts. Work 3 rows garter st.

Next row (RS): begin diagonal pat (Chart I) as given for Front hem band. When you have completed 9 rows of diagonal pat, work 3 rows garter st.

Inner collar, Next row (RS): purl.

Next row (WS): p13 (13, 14, 14), p2tog, *p26 (26, 28, 28), p2tog*, rep from * once more, p13 (13, 14, 14), to 81 (81, 87, 87) sts. Work 12 more rows in st st, then bind off all sts very loosely.

Sew left shoulder seam and collar seam. Using a loose whipstitch seam to allow for stretch, sew the bound-off edge in position.

Sew tops of sleeves to armholes between armhole bind offs. Sew upper sides of sleeves to armhole bind offs. Sew remaining sleeve seams and side seams. 🍁

skyward

Look up on a sunny fall afternoon, and you'll see blazing orange, green, and gold leaves against that deep blue hue the sky takes on in autumn. To bring texture to the vibrant mix of fall colors in this pullover and purse, I added a long-haired orange yarn in the Fair Isle sections and a simple knot stitch (less work than popcorn stitches) in the plain areas. Try substituting your own colors, too – perhaps icy pale blues and lavenders, or warm lodens and rusts.

SKILL LEVEL: INTERMEDIATE

MEASUREMENTS

SIZES (in inches)	TEENS			WOMEN			
	12	14	16	SM	MD	LG	XL
Finished Bust	35	37	40	42	44½	47	49
Finished Length	20	21	22	23	23½	25	26

MATERIALS

Yarn: MC, A, B, C – Patons Classic Merino 100% Wool (221 yds or 204 m/100 gr ball). D – Katia Technofur 100% Tactel Polyamide (112 yds or 103 m/50 gr ball) used with two strands of yarn held together as one. *See also page 126 for yarn information.*

NO. OF BALLS	TEENS			WOMEN			
	12	14	16	SM	MD	LG	XL
MC: Blueberry #213	4	5	5	6	6	7	7
A: Old Gold #204	1	1	1	1	1	1	1
B: Leaf Green #240	1	1	1	2	2	2	2
C: Dusky Blue #214	1	1	1	1	1	1	1
D: Orange Mix #400	2	2	2	3	3	3	3

Needles: 1 pr. U.S. size 7 (4.5 mm) needles OR SIZE TO OBTAIN GAUGE

Spare needles or stitch holders

SPECIAL ABBREVIATIONS

KS = Knot Stitch: k1, p1, k1, p1, k1 all in next st. Sl next-to-last-worked st over last-worked st 4 times.

GAUGE

20 sts and 26 rows= 4" in st st and charted pattern

To work Gauge Swatch: with MC, cast on 24 sts and work Rows 1 through 14 of the Fair Isle charted pat on page 28, working the 6-st repeat 4 times across row. Knit RS rows and purl WS rows, reading RS rows of chart from right to left and WS rows from left to right, and carrying unused color across WS. Note that D (Orange Mix) is worked with two strands of yarn held together as one. Change to MC and work st st until piece measures 6" from bottom edge. Bind off. Block swatch by laying it flat and applying lots of steam with steam iron held just above the swatch. Let cool and dry. The gauge above applies to both st st and Fair Isle sections. If you have too many sts or rows to the inch, switch to a larger needle; too few means you should use a smaller needle.

Your garment will not fit properly if the tension gauge is incorrect! Take the time to check by making gauge swatch.

Directions are given for Teens' size 12. Teens' sizes 14 and 16, and Women's sizes Small, Medium, Large, and Extra-Large are given in parentheses. Where there is only one number, it applies to all sizes.

LOWER FRONT

With MC, cast on 87 (93, 99, 105, 111, 117, 123) sts.

Work ribbing as follows:

RS rows: p3, *k3, p3*, rep from * to end.

WS rows: k3, *p3, k3*, rep from * to end.

Rep the last 2 rows of ribbing until piece measures 3" long, ending with RS facing for next row.

Begin Knot stitch pat:

Rows 1 and 5: knit.

Rows 2, 4, and 6: purl.

Row 3: k7, *KS, k5*, k2, rep from * to end.

Row 7: k6, *KS, k5*, rep from * to last 3 sts, k3.

Row 8: purl.

Rep these 8 rows to form Knot Stitch pat.

UPPER FRONT

Continue in Knot Stitch pat until piece measures 9 (10, 11, 11, 11½, 12, 12½)" from bottom edge, ending with either Row 2 or Row 6 of pat and increasing 3 sts purlwise evenly across last row, to 90 (96, 102, 108, 114, 120, 126) sts.

Begin charted pat (RS): Work Row 1 of Chart, repeating 6-st repeat 15 (16, 17, 18, 19, 20, 21) times across row and following guidelines in Gauge Swatch on page 27 for working Fair Isle.

Work through rows of chart until piece measures 10½ (11, 11½, 12, 12, 12½, 13)" from bottom edge, ending with RS facing for next row.

- MC
- A
- B
- C
- D

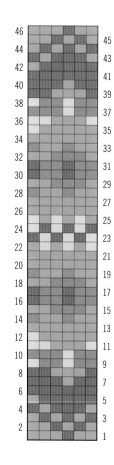

Raglan shaping: Bind off first 6 sts at beginning of next 2 rows, working in pat as established to end. You should now have 78 (84, 90, 96, 102, 108, 114) sts remaining. Bind off first st at beg of every row 20 (23, 25, 27, 28, 29, 32) times per side, continuing in charted pat as established until chart is complete; thereafter work st st in MC. Work even, if necessary, until piece measures 1½ (1½, 1½, 2½, 2½, 3, 3½)" from last row of chart, ending with RS facing for next row. Sl remaining 38 (38, 40, 42, 46, 50, 50) sts to spare needle or stitch holder.

BACK

Work exactly as given for Front to "Raglan shaping."

Raglan shaping: bind off first 3 sts at beginning of next 2 rows, working in pat as established to end. You should now have 84 (90, 96, 102, 108, 114, 120) sts remaining. Bind off first st at beg of every row 23 (26, 28, 30, 31, 32, 35) times per side, continuing in charted pat as established until chart is complete; thereafter work st st in MC. Work even, if necessary, until piece measures 2½ (2½, 2½, 3½, 3½, 4, 4½)" from last row of chart, ending with RS facing for next row. Sl remaining 38 (38, 40, 42, 46, 50, 50) sts to spare needle or stitch holder.

LEFT SLEEVE

With MC, cast on 54 (54, 60, 66, 66, 72, 72) sts and work rib as follows: *k3, p3*, rep from * to end. Rep last row until piece measures 4" from bottom edge, ending with RS facing for next row.

Begin Knot Stitch pat:

Rows 1 and 5: knit.

Rows 2, 4, and 6: purl.

Row 3: k4, *KS, k5*, rep from * to last 2 sts, k2.

Row 7: k3, *KS, k5*, rep from * to last 3 sts, k3.

Row 8: purl.

Rep the last 8 rows to form Knot Stitch pat; AT THE SAME TIME, inc 1 st at each side every 6th row until you have 66 (72, 78, 84, 84, 90, 96) sts. Work your incs in Knot Stitch pat.

Work even, if necessary, until piece measures 13½ (14, 15½, 15, 16, 16½, 16½)" from bottom edge, ending with either Row 2 or Row 6 of patt.

Begin charted pat (RS): work Row 1 of chart 11 (12, 13, 14, 14, 15, 16) times across row.

Work through rows of chart until chart is complete; thereafter work st st in MC; AT THE SAME TIME, when piece measures 15 (15, 16, 16, 16½, 16½, 17)" from bottom edge, begin shaping sleeve cap on the next RS row as follows:

Raglan shaping (RS): bind off 3 sts at beginning of row, work in charted pat as established to end.

Next row (WS): bind off 6 sts, work in pat to end. Hereafter, bind off first st at beginning of every row until you have 17 (17, 19, 21, 19, 23, 23) sts remaining.

Work even, if necessary, until length of raglan edge matches length of Front raglan edge, ending with RS facing for next row.

Next row (RS): work short row shaping: bind off first st, k11 (11, 13, 15, 13, 15, 15). Bring yarn to front, sl next st, bring yarn to back, return slipped st to left-hand needle. Turn, leaving remaining sts on left-hand needle.

Next row (WS): purl.

Next row (RS): bind off first st, k8 (8, 10, 11, 10, 12, 12). Bring yarn to front, sl next st, bring yarn to back, return slipped st to left-hand needle. Turn, leaving remaining sts on left-hand needle.

Next row (WS): purl.

Next row (RS): bind off first st, k5 (5, 7, 7, 7, 8, 8). Bring yarn to front, sl next st, bring yarn to back, return slipped st to left-hand needle. Turn, leaving remaining sts on left-hand needle.

Next row (WS): purl.

Sl remaining 14 (14, 16, 18, 16, 20, 20) sts to spare needle or stitch holder.

RIGHT SLEEVE

Work as for Left Sleeve to "Raglan shaping."

Raglan shaping (RS): bind off 6 sts at beginning of row, work in charted pat as established to end.

Next row (WS): bind off 3 sts, work in pat to end. Hereafter, bind off first st at beginning of every row until you have 17 (17, 19, 21, 19, 23, 23) sts remaining.

Work even, if necessary, until length of raglan edge matches length of Front raglan edge, ending with WS facing for next row.

Next row (WS): work short row shaping: bind off first st, p11 (11, 13, 15, 13, 15, 15). Bring yarn to back, sl next st, bring yarn to front, return slipped st to left-hand needle. Turn, leaving remaining sts on left-hand needle.

Next row (RS): knit.

Next row (WS): bind off first st, p8 (8, 10, 11, 10, 12, 12). Bring yarn to back, sl next st, bring yarn to front, return slipped st to left-hand needle. Turn, leaving remaining sts on left-hand needle.

Next row (RS): knit.

Next row (WS): bind off first st, p5 (5, 7, 7, 7, 8, 8). Bring yarn to back, sl next st, bring yarn to front, return slipped st to left-hand needle. Turn, leaving remaining sts on left-hand needle. Sl remaining 14 (14, 16, 18, 16, 20, 20) sts to spare needle or stitch holder.

FINISHING

Sew sleeve seams and side seams.

Set in right sleeve, with longer raglan edge of sleeve matched to longer back raglan edge. Sew in left sleeve along shorter front raglan edge only, leaving back raglan seam open.

Collar: with RS of garment facing and MC, transfer 14 (14, 16, 18, 16, 20, 20) sts from left sleeve holder, 38 (38, 40, 42, 46, 50, 50) sts from Front neck edge holder, 14 (14, 16, 18, 16, 20, 20) sts from right sleeve holder, and 38 (38, 40, 42, 46, 50, 50) sts from Back neck edge holder to needles. You should have a total of 104 (104, 112, 120, 124, 140, 140) sts.

Next row (WS): p and dec 2 (2, 4, 6, 4, 8, 8) sts evenly across row to 102 (102, 108, 114, 120, 132, 132) sts. Work k3, p3 ribbing as given for Sleeves until collar measures 6" from bottom edge, ending with RS facing for next row. Bind off loosely in pat.

Sew left back raglan seam and collar seam, reversing collar seam at upper half of collar if you prefer to wear it folded down.

PURSE *(make 2 pieces)*

With MC, cast on 36 sts. Work 6 rows k3, p3 ribbing as given for Left Sleeve. Begin Chart, working Row 1 of Chart 6 times across row.

Work through the 46 rows of chart until chart is complete; thereafter work 4 rows st st in MC. Bind off.

Sew side and bottom edges of purse pieces together, leaving ribbed edges open at top.

Tassels (make 2): wind MC 20 times around short edge of a small paperback book (approx. 4" or 5" wide). Break yarn, leaving a long tail and slip tail through all loops at top fold and tie tightly. Slip book out and wind tail tightly around tassel loops about 3/4" down from top fold; fasten tightly. Use end to stitch tassel to bottom corner of purse. Trim tassel ends to desired length.

Cord: cut 9 strands of yarn, each approx. 2 yards long. Tie all ends together at one end. Group strands into three groups of 3 strands each and braid together until braid is 42" long. Knot ends and trim. Sew ends of cord to upper inside corners of purse. 🍁

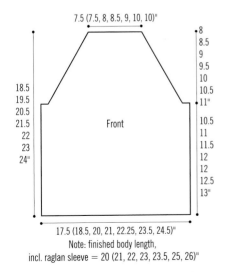

7.5 (7.5, 8, 8.5, 9, 10, 10)"

8
8.5
9
9.5
10
10.5
11"

18.5
19.5
20.5
21.5
22
23
24"

Front

10.5
11
11.5
12
12
12.5
13"

17.5 (18.5, 20, 21, 22.25, 23.5, 24.5)"
Note: finished body length,
incl. raglan sleeve = 20 (21, 22, 23, 23.5, 25, 26)"

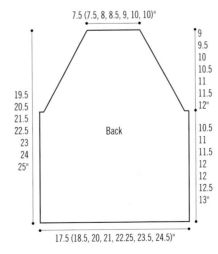

7.5 (7.5, 8, 8.5, 9, 10, 10)"

9
9.5
10
10.5
11
11.5
12"

19.5
20.5
21.5
22.5
23
24
25"

Back

10.5
11
11.5
12
12
12.5
13"

17.5 (18.5, 20, 21, 22.25, 23.5, 24.5)"

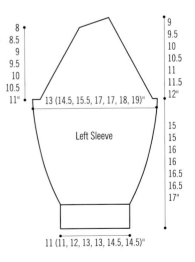

8
8.5
9
9.5
10
10.5
11"

9
9.5
10
10.5
11
11.5
12"

13 (14.5, 15.5, 17, 17, 18, 19)"

Left Sleeve

15
15
16
16
16.5
16.5
17"

11 (11, 12, 13, 13, 14.5, 14.5)"

spark

A simple garter stitch rib makes a canvas on which I can play with color combinations.
A sportswear-influenced colorway is shown on the finished sweater at left, and the swatches
shown on page 32 may give you inspiration as well. You could make this wear-everywhere basic
with a turtleneck as shown or use the crew-neck option also given in the pattern.

SKILL LEVEL: VERY EASY

MEASUREMENTS

SIZES (in inches)	TEENS			ADULTS			
	12	14	16	SM	MD	LG	XL
Finished Chest	34	37	40	43	46	50	53
Finished Length	22	23½	24	25½	26	26½	27

MATERIALS

Yarn: Patons Classic Merino 100% Wool (221 yds or
204 m/100 gr ball). *See also page 126 for yarn information.*

NO. OF BALLS	TEENS			ADULTS			
	12	14	16	SM	MD	LG	XL
MC: Navy #216	3	3	3	4	4	5	5
A: Purple #212	1	1	2	2	2	3	3
B: Paprika #238	1	1	2	2	2	2	2
C: Blueberry #213	1	1	2	2	2	3	3
D: Leaf Green #240	1	1	1	1	1	1	1

Needles: 1 pr. U.S. size 7 (4.5 mm) needles OR SIZE TO
OBTAIN GAUGE

Spare needle or stitch holder

GAUGE

20 sts and 28 rows = 4" in garter rib pattern

To work Gauge Swatch: with MC, cast on 28 sts and work
garter rib pat as follows:

RS rows: k4, *p4, k4*, rep from * to end.

WS rows: purl.

Rep the last 2 rows until piece measures 4" from bottom edge.
Bind off in pat (bind off knit sts knitwise and bind off purl sts
purlwise). Block swatch by laying flat and applying lots of
steam with steam iron held just above the swatch. Let cool and
dry. If you have too many sts and rows to the inch, switch to a
larger needle; too few means you should use a smaller needle.

*Your garment will not fit properly if the tension gauge is
incorrect! Take the time to check by making gauge swatch.*

*Directions are given for Teens' size 12. Teens' sizes 14 and
16, and Adults' sizes Small, Medium, Large, and Extra-Large
are given in parentheses. Where there is only one number, it
applies to all sizes.*

FRONT

With MC, cast on 84 (92, 100, 108, 116, 124, 132) sts.

Work rib pat as given for Gauge Swatch; AT THE SAME TIME,
work stripe sequence as follows:

With MC, work 12 rows.

With A, work 6 rows.

With B, work 4 rows.

With C, work 6 rows.

With MC, work 4 rows.

With D, work 2 rows.

Rep the last 34 rows until piece measures 14½ (15½, 15½,
16½, 16½, 16½, 16½)" from bottom edge, ending with RS
facing for next row.

Armhole shaping: Bind off first 8 sts, then work in pat to end
on each of the next 2 rows. You should now have 68 (76, 84,
92, 100, 108, 116) sts remaining.

Continue in pat until piece measures 19½ (21, 21½, 22½, 23, 23½, 24)" from bottom edge, ending with RS facing for next row.

Neck shaping: keeping in pat as established, work 28 (32, 36, 38, 42, 46, 50) sts. Sl next 12 (12, 12, 16, 16, 16, 16) sts to holder. Join 2nd ball of same color to next st and work in pat to end. Working both sides at same time with separate balls of yarn and keeping in stripe sequence and rib pat as established, work neck shaping as follows:

Row 1 (WS): on right neck edge, work to last 2 sts, k2tog (or p2tog, to keep in pat). On left neck edge, bind off 3 (4, 4, 5, 5, 5, 5) sts, work in pat to end.

Row 2 (RS): rep Row 1.

Row 3 (WS): on right neck edge, work to last 2 sts, k2tog (or p2tog, to keep in pat). On left neck edge, bind off 3 sts, work in pat to end.

Row 4 (RS): rep Row 3.

Row 5 (WS): on right neck edge, work to last 2 sts, k2tog (or p2tog, to keep in pat). On left neck edge, bind off 1 st, work in pat to end.

Row 6 (RS): rep Row 5.

Rep last 2 rows 0 (1, 1, 1, 1, 1, 2) more time(s). You should now have 18 (20, 24, 26, 30, 34, 36) sts remaining for each shoulder.

Work even (no more decs) until piece measures 22 (23½, 24, 25½, 26, 26½, 27)" from bottom edge, ending with RS facing for next row.

Bind off all remaining sts in pat.

BACK

Work as for Front, up to "Neck shaping." Work even until piece matches length of Front to shoulder, ending with RS facing for next row.

Bind off 18 (20, 24, 26, 30, 34, 36) sts at beginning of next 2 rows. Leave remaining 32 (36, 36, 40, 40, 40, 44) sts for Back neck on spare needle or holder.

SLEEVES

Note: read through sleeve directions before proceeding.

With MC, cast on 36 (36, 36, 36, 44, 44, 44) sts.

Work rib pat as given for Gauge Swatch on page 31; at the same time, work same stripe sequence as given for Front.

Rep stripe pat; AT THE SAME TIME, inc 1 st at each side on 3rd row and then every following 4th row as follows: keeping in pat as established, work 1 st, inc 1, work pat to last 2 sts, inc 1, work last st. Make your incs either knitwise or purlwise to keep continuity of rib pat.

When you have increased to 40 (40, 44, 56, 56, 68, 72) sts, begin working incs every 6th row until you have a total of 74 (80, 84, 90, 94, 100, 104) sts.

Work even (no incs) until piece measures 20½ (21, 21½, 22, 22½, 22½, 23)" from bottom edge, ending with RS facing for next row.

Bind off all sts in pat.

FINISHING

Sew right shoulder seam.

Turtleneck collar: with RS facing and MC, pick up and knit 18 (20, 20, 20, 20, 20, 22) sts along left Front neck edge, knit across 12 (12, 12, 16, 16, 16, 16) sts from center Front st holder, pick up and knit 18 (20, 20, 20, 20, 20, 22) sts along right Front neck edge, knit across 32 (36, 36, 40, 40, 40, 44) sts from Back neck st holder. You should have a total of 80 (88, 88, 96, 96, 96, 104) sts for collar.

Work collar in stripe sequence as given for Front, establishing rib placement as follows:

WS rows: purl.

RS rows: p2 (4, 4, 0, 0, 0, 0), k4 (4, 4, 2, 2, 2, 4), *p4, k4*, rep from * to last 2 (0, 0, 6, 6, 6, 4) sts, p2 (0, 0, 4, 4, 4, 4), k0 (0, 0, 2, 2, 2, 0).

Rep the last 2 rows 8 more times.

Next row (WS): keeping in rib pat as established, work rib pat on WS rows and purl on RS rows, so that rib pat is visible when collar is folded down. When collar measures 5½" from bottom edge, bind off all sts in pat.

Optional crewneck collar: With MC, pick up sts as given for Turtleneck collar and work 6 rows in rib as given for turtleneck. Bind off in pat.

Sew left shoulder seam and collar seam (reversing seam at outer half of collar for fold-back of turtleneck). Sew tops of sleeves to armholes between armhole bind offs. Sew upper sides of sleeves to armhole bind offs. Sew remaining sleeve seams and side seams.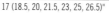

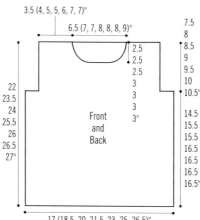

3.5 (4, 5, 5, 6, 7, 7)"
6.5 (7, 7, 8, 8, 8, 9)"
7.5
8
2.5 — 8.5
2.5 — 9
2.5 — 9.5
3 — 10
3 — 10.5"
22
23.5
3
24 — 14.5
25.5 — Front 3"
26 and 15.5
26.5 Back 15.5
27" 16.5
16.5
16.5
16.5"
17 (18.5, 20, 21.5, 23, 25, 26.5)"

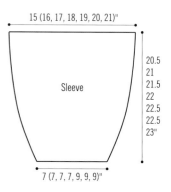

15 (16, 17, 18, 19, 20, 21)"
20.5
21
21.5
Sleeve 22
22.5
22.5
23"
7 (7, 7, 7, 9, 9, 9)"

siobhan

This sweater has been a favorite of my readers since I first designed it. Although it's complex, with the Celtic-inspired knotwork and arrowhead cables at the yoke and the bobbled diamond cables at lower body and sleeves, it seems to satisfy a craving for something different! For this book, I have added a teen's size 16 and a longer version (which many of you requested).

SKILL LEVEL: EXPERIENCED

MEASUREMENTS

SIZES (in inches)	TEENS	WOMEN			
	16	SM	MD	LG	XL
Finished Bust	36	39	42	45	48
Finished Length					
Long Version	22	22½	22½	23	23
Short Version	17	17½	17½	18	18

MATERIALS

Yarn, Long Version: Patons Classic Merino 100% Wool #202 (221 yds or 204 m/100 gr ball).
Yarn, Short Version: Patons Classic Merino 100% Wool #238 (221 yds or 204 m/100 gr ball).
See also page 126 for yarn information.

NO. OF BALLS	TEENS	WOMEN			
	16	SM	MD	LG	XL
Long Version, #202	6	6	7	7	8
Short Version, #238	5	5	6	6	7

Needles: 1 pr. each U.S. sizes 6 and 7 (4 mm and 4.5 mm) needles OR SIZE TO FIT GAUGE

Stitch markers (you can use loops of contrasting yarn)

Cable needle

SPECIAL ABBREVIATIONS

MB = Make Bobble: inc 1 in the next st, turn work and inc 1 purlwise, inc 1 purlwise. Turn again and k4. Turn again and p2tog, p2tog. Turn again and p2tog.

cn = cable needle

GAUGE

20 sts and 26 rows= 4" in st st using larger needles

To work Gauge Swatch: using larger needles, cast on 24 stitches and work st st until piece measures 4" from bottom edge, then bind off all sts. Block swatch by laying flat and applying lots of steam with steam iron held just above the swatch. Let cool and dry. If you have too many sts and rows to the inch, switch to a larger needle; too few means you should use a smaller needle.

Your garment will not fit properly if the tension gauge is incorrect! Take the time to check by making gauge swatch.

Directions are given for Teens' size 16. Womens' sizes Small, Medium, Large, and Extra-Large are given in parentheses. (Due to the large size of pattern repeat, neither Teens' size 12 nor Teens' size 14 is given for this pattern.) Where there is only one number, it applies to all sizes.

FRONT – LOWER BODY

With smaller needles, cast on 100 (108, 116, 124, 132) sts and work seed-stitch band as follows:

First row (RS): *k1, p1*, rep from * to end.

Following rows: k the p sts and p the k sts.

Work seed stitch for a total of five rows.

Change to larger needles and work Diamond Cable pattern for lower body.

DIAMOND CABLE PATTERN – CHARTED INSTRUCTIONS

Row 1 (WS): k8 (12, 16, 20, 24), work Row 1 of Diamond Cable chart on page 37 as follows: work the 27-st repeat twice, then work across full row of chart, k8 (12, 16, 20, 24).

RS rows: p8 (12, 16, 20, 24), work across Row 2 of Diamond Cable chart, then work the 27-st repeat twice more, p8 (12, 16, 20, 24).

Pattern placement is now established. Work through to last row of Diamond Cable chart. Repeat Rows 1 through 16 twice more for short version or 4 times more for long version, then work Rows 1 through 6 once more, thus ending with WS facing for next row. Skip to "Yoke."

DIAMOND CABLE PATTERN – WRITTEN INSTRUCTIONS

Row 1 (WS): k8 (12, 16, 20, 24), placing marker on last st, p3, *k7, p2, k6, p2, k7, p3*, rep from * twice more, place marker after next st and k8 (12, 16, 20, 24).

Row 2 (RS): p to marker, [sl 1, k2, psso the last 2 knitted sts], *p7, k2, p6, k2, p7, [sl 1, k2, psso the last 2 knitted sts]*, rep from * twice more, p to end.

Row 3 (WS): k to marker, p1, yo, p1, *k7, p2, k6, p2, k7, p1, yo, p1*, rep from * twice more, k to end.

Row 4 (RS): p to marker, k3, *p7, [sl 2 to cn and hold to front, p1, k2 from cn], p4, [sl 1 to cn and hold to back, k2, p1 from cn], p7, k3*, rep from * twice more, p to end.

Row 5 (WS): k to marker, p3, *k8, p2, k4, p2, k8, p3*, rep from * twice more, k to end.

Row 6 (RS): p to marker, [sl 1, k2, psso last 2 knitted sts], *p8, [sl 2 to cn and hold to front, p1, k2 from cn], p2, [sl 1 to cn and hold to back, k2, p1 from cn], p8, [sl 1, k2, psso last 2]*, rep from * twice more, p to end.

Row 7 (WS): k to marker, p1, yo, p1, *k9, p2, k2, p2, k9, p1, yo, p1*, rep from * twice more, k to end.

Row 8 (RS): p to marker, k3, *p9, [sl 2 to cn and hold to front, p1, k2 from cn], [sl 1 to cn and hold to back, k2, p1 from cn], p9, k3*, rep from * twice more, p to end.

Row 9 (WS): k to marker, p3, *k10, p4, k10, p3*, rep from * twice more, k to end.

Row 10 (RS): p to marker, [sl 1, k2, psso last 2], *p5, MB, p4, [sl 2 to cn and hold to front, k2, k2 from cn], p4, MB, p5, [sl 1, k2, psso last 2]*, rep from * twice more, p to end.

Row 11 (WS): k to marker, p1, yo, p1, *k10, p4, k10, p1, yo, p1*, rep from * twice more, k to end.

Row 12 (RS): p to marker, k3, *p9, [sl 1 to cn and hold to back, k2, p1 from cn], [sl 2 to cn and hold to front, p1, k2 from cn], p9, k3*, rep from * twice more, p to end.

Row 13 (WS): k to marker, p3, *k9, p2, k2, p2, k9, p3*, rep from * twice more, k to end.

Row 14 (RS): p to marker, [sl 1, k2, psso last 2], *p8, [sl 1 to cn and hold to back, k2, p1 from cn], p2, [sl 2 to cn and hold to front, p1, k2 from cn], p8, [sl 1, k2, psso last 2]*, rep from * twice more, p to end.

Row 15 (WS): k to marker, p1, yo, p1, *k8, p2, k4, p2, k8, p1, yo, p1*, rep from * twice more, k to end.

Row 16 (RS): p to marker, k3,*p7, [sl 1 to cn and hold to back, k2, p1 from cn], p4, [sl 2 to cn and hold to front, p1, k2 from cn], p7, k3*, rep from * twice more, p to end.

Repeat Rows 1 through 16 twice more for short version or 4 more times for long version, then work Rows 1 through 6 once more, thus ending with WS facing for next row. Remove stitch markers.

YOKE

Note: read the following, through Neck shaping, before beginning the yoke.

Hereafter, follow charted or written Yoke instructions, working armhole shaping as indicated. AT THE SAME TIME, when piece measures 5 (5½, 5½, 6, 6)" from beginning of armhole shaping, work "Neck shaping" as indicated.

Note: Due to decreases in pat, after completing the armhole shaping and arrowhead cables, you should have 74 (76, 84, 92, 96) sts remaining.)

Neck shaping: work across 31 (32, 36, 40, 42) sts and tie on second ball. With second ball, bind off next 12 sts, then work in pat to end.

Working both sides at same time with separate balls of yarn and keeping in yoke pat, bind off sts at beginning of each neck edge row in the following sequence: bind off 5 (5, 7, 7, 7) sts at each side of neck edge once; bind off 4 sts at each side of neck edge once; bind off 2 sts at each side of neck edge once; bind off 1 st at each side of neck edge as many times as needed until you have 16 (17, 19, 23, 25) sts remaining at each shoulder.

Work even in yoke pat, if necessary, until piece measures 7½ (8, 8, 8½, 8½)" from beginning of armhole shaping, ending with RS facing for next row. Bind off all sts in pat.

CHARTED INSTRUCTIONS

Row 1 (WS): beginning at left side of Yoke chart, work Row 1, repeating panel pat 3 times, then working to end of charted row.

Row 2 (RS): beginning at right side of Yoke chart, work Row 2, repeating panel pat 3 times, then working to end of charted row.

Pattern placement is now established. Work through to last row of chart, noting that on Row 30, replace "MB" with "p1" on third panel pat repeat. Repeat Rows 31 through 52 to top of Front, AT THE SAME TIME, follow Neck shaping and completion directions as given above.

Row 1 (WS): k3 (7, 11, 15, 19), *k2, p2, k1, p1, yo, p1, k1, p2, k6, p2, k2, p2, k4*, rep from * twice more, k2, p2, k1, p1, yo, p1, k1, p2, k5 (9, 13, 17, 21).

Row 2 (RS): p3 (7, 11, 15, 19), *p1, [sl 1 to cn, hold to back, k2, p1 from cn], p1, k3, p1, [sl 2 to cn and hold to front, p1, k2 from cn], p5, [sl 2 to cn and hold to front, p1, k2 from cn], [sl 1 to cn, hold to back, k2, p1 from cn], p4*, rep from * twice more, p1, [sl 1 to cn, hold to back, k2, p1 from cn], p1, k3, p1, [sl 2 to cn and hold to front, p1, k2 from cn], p4 (8, 12, 16, 20).

Row 3 (WS): k3 (7, 11, 15, 19), *k1, p2, k2, p3, k2, p2, k6, p4, k5*, rep from * twice more, k1, p2, k2, p3, k2, p2, k4 (8, 12, 16, 20).

Row 4 (RS): p3 (7, 11, 15, 19), *[sl 1 to cn and hold to back, k2, p1 from cn], p2, [sl 1, k2, psso last 2], p2, [sl 2 to cn and hold to front, p1, k2 from cn], p5, [sl 1, k1, psso], k2tog, p5*, rep from * twice more, [sl 1 to cn and hold to back, k2, p1 from cn], p2, [sl 1, k2, psso last 2], p2, [sl 2 to cn and hold to front, p1, k2 from cn], p3 (7, 11, 15, 19).

Row 5 (WS): k3 (7, 11, 15, 19), *p2, k3, p1, yo, p1, k3, p2, k5, p2, k5*, rep from * twice more, p2, k3, p1, yo, p1, k3, p2, k3 (7, 11, 15, 19).

Row 6 (RS): p3 (7, 11, 15, 19), *k2, p3, k3, p3, k2, p5, [sl 1, k1, psso], p5*, rep from * twice more, k2, p3, k3, p3, k2, p3 (7, 11, 15, 19). You should now have 91 (99, 107, 115, 123) sts remaining.

Row 7 (WS): k3 (7, 11, 15, 19), *p2, k3, p3, k3, p2, k11*, rep from * twice more, p2, k3, p3, k3, p2, k3 (7, 11, 15, 19).

Row 8 (RS): bind off 2 (3, 3, 3, 3) sts, p0 (3, 7, 11, 15), *[sl 2 to cn and hold to front, p1, k2 from cn], p2, [sl 1, k2, psso last 2], p2, [sl 1 to cn and hold to back, k2, p1 from cn], p11*, rep from * twice more, [sl 2 to cn and hold to front, p1, k2 from cn], p2, [sl 1, k2, psso last 2], p2, [sl 1 to cn and hold to back, k2, p1 from cn], p3 (7, 11, 15, 19).

Row 9 (WS): bind off 2 (3, 3, 3, 3) sts, k1 (4, 8, 12, 16) *p2, k2, p1, yo, p1, k2, p2, k13*, rep from * twice more, p2, k2, p1, yo, p1, k2, p2, k2 (5, 9, 13, 17).

Row 10 (RS): bind off 1 (1, 1, 1, 2), p0 (3, 7, 11, 14), *[sl 2 to cn and hold to front, p1, k2 from cn], p1, k3, p1, [sl 1 to cn and hold to back, k2, p1 from cn], p6, MB, p6*, rep from * twice more, [sl 2 to cn and hold to front, p1, k2 from cn], p1, k3, p1, [sl 1 to cn and hold to back, k2, p1 from cn], p2 (5, 9, 13, 17).

Row 11 (WS): bind off 1 (1, 1, 1, 2), k1 (4, 8, 12, 15), * p2, k1, p3, k1, p2, k15*, rep from * twice more, p2, k1, p3, k1, p2, k2 (5, 9, 13, 16).

Row 12 (RS): bind off 1 (1, 1, 1, 2), p0 (3, 7, 11, 13), *[sl 2 to cn and hold to front, p1, k2 from cn], [sl 1, k2, psso last 2], [sl 1 to cn and hold to back, k2, p1 from cn], p7, k1, p7*, rep from * twice more, [sl 2 to cn and hold to front, p1, k2 from cn], [sl 1, k2, psso last 2], [sl 1 to cn and hold to back, k2, p1 from cn], p2 (5, 9, 13, 16).

Row 13 (WS): bind off 1 (1, 1, 1, 2), k1 (4, 8, 12, 14), *p3, yo, p3, k8, inc 1 purlwise, k8*, rep from * twice more, p3, yo, p3, k2 (5, 9, 13, 15).

Row 14 (RS): bind off 0 (1, 1, 1, 1), p2 (3, 7, 11, 13), *[sl 2 to cn and hold to front, p1, k2 from cn], k1, [sl 1 to cn and hold to back, k2, p1 from cn], p5, MB, p2, inc 1 knitwise, inc 1 knitwise, p2, MB, p5*, rep from * twice more, [sl 2 to cn and hold to front, p1, k2 from cn], k1, [sl 1 to cn and hold to back, k2, p1 from cn], p2 (5, 9, 13, 15).

Row 15 (WS): bind off 0 (1, 1, 1, 1), k3 (4, 8, 12, 14), *p5, k8, [sl 1 to cn and hold to front, p2, k1 from cn], [sl 2 to cn and hold to back, k1, p2 from cn], k8*, rep from * twice more, p5, k3 (5, 9, 13, 15).

Row 16 (RS): bind off 1 st, p1 (3, 7, 11, 13), *[sl 1, k1, psso], k1, k2tog, p7, [sl 1 to cn and hold to back, k2, p1 from cn], p2, [sl 2 to cn and hold to front, p1, k2 from cn], p7*, rep from * twice more, [sl 1, k1, psso], k1, k2tog, p3 (5, 9, 13, 15).

Row 17 (WS): bind off 1, k1 (3, 7, 11, 13), *p3, k6, [sl 1 to cn and hold to front, p2, k1 from cn], k4, [sl 2 to cn and hold to back, k1, p2 from cn], k6*, rep from * twice more, p3, k2 (4, 8, 12, 14).

Row 18 (RS): bind off 0 (1, 1, 1, 1), p2 (2, 6, 10, 12), *[sl 1, k2tog, psso], p3, MB, p1, [sl 1 to cn and hold to back, k2, p1 from cn], p6, [sl 2 to cn and hold to front, p1, k2 from cn], p1, MB, p3*, rep from * twice more, [sl 1, k2tog, psso] p2 (4, 8, 12, 14).

Row 19 (WS): bind off 0 (1, 1, 1, 1), k2 (2, 6, 10, 12), *k6, p2, [k3, p2] twice, k5*, rep from * twice more, k3 (4, 8, 12, 14). You should now have 74 (76, 84, 92, 96) sts.

Row 20 (RS): p3 (4, 8, 12, 14), *p4, [sl 1 to cn and hold to back, k2, p1 from cn], p2, [sl 2 to cn and hold to front, k2, k2 from cn], p2, [sl 2 to cn and hold to front, p1, k2 from cn], p5*, rep from * twice more, p3 (4, 8, 12, 14).

Row 21 (WS): k2 (3, 7, 11, 13), *k5, p2, k3, p4, k3, p2, k4*, rep from * twice more, p3 (4, 8, 12, 14).

Legend

- ☐ k on RS, p on WS
- ⊟ p on RS, k on WS
- ⊡ MB: make bobble (see Special Abbreviations)
- ⊙ yarn over
- ⊠ sl 1, k1, psso
- ⊿ k2tog
- ▨ no stitch
- ⊼ double dec: sl 1, k2tog, psso
- ⅄ inc 1 knitwise on RS rows or purlwise on WS rows
- ⬠ sl 1 to cn & hold to front, p1, k1 from cn
- ⬠ sl 1 to cn & hold to back, k1, p1 from cn
- ⬠ sl 2 to cn & hold to front, k1, k2 from cn
- ⬠ sl 1 to cn & hold to back, k2, k1 from cn
- ⬠ RS rows: sl 2 to cn & hold to front, p1, k2 from cn
  WS rows: sl 1 to cn & hold to front, p2, k1 from cn
- ⬠ RS rows: sl 1 to cn & hold to back, k2, p1 from cn
  WS rows: sl 2 to cn & hold to back, k1, p2 from cn
- ⬡ sl1, k2, psso last 2 sts
- ⬠ sl 2 to cn & hold to front, k2, k2 from cn
- ⬠ sl 2 to cn & hold to back, k2, k2 from cn

Note: "cn" = cable needle

Yoke Chart

*On Row 30, replace MB on 3rd panel pat rep with p1.

Diamond Cable Chart

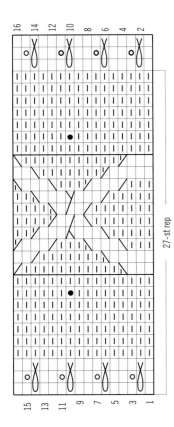

27-st rep

Row 22 (RS): p3 (4, 8, 12, 14), *p3, [sl 1 to cn and hold to back, k2, p1 from cn], p2, [sl 1 to cn and hold to back, k2, p1 from cn], [sl 2 to cn and hold to front, p1, k2 from cn], p2, [sl 2 to cn and hold to front, p1, k2 from cn], p4*, rep from * twice more, p2 (3, 7, 11, 13).

Row 23 (WS): k2 (3, 7, 11, 13), *k4, p2, k3, p2, k2, [p2, k3] twice*, rep from * twice more, k to end.

Row 24 (RS): p3 (4, 8, 12, 14), *p1, MB, p1, k2, p2, [sl 1 to cn and hold to back, k2, p1 from cn], p2, [sl 2 to cn and hold to front, p1, k2 from cn], p2, k2, p1, MB, p2*, rep from * twice more, p to end.

Row 25 (WS): k2 (3, 7, 11, 13), *k4, p2, k2, p2, k4, p2, k2, p2, k3*, rep from * twice more, k to end.

Row 26 (RS): p3 (4, 8, 12, 14), *p2, [sl 1 to cn and hold to back, k2, p1 from cn], p2, k2, p4, k2, p2, [sl 2 to cn and hold to front, p1, k2 from cn], p3*, rep from * twice more, p to end.

Row 27 (WS): k2 (3, 7, 11, 13), *[k3, p2] twice, k4, p2, k3, p2, k2*, rep from * twice more, k to end.

Row 28 (RS): p3 (4, 8, 12, 14), *p2, k2, p3, [sl 2 to cn and hold to front, k1, k2 from cn], p2, [sl 1 to cn and hold to back, k2, k1 from cn], p3, k2, p3*, rep from * twice more, p to end.

Row 29 (WS): k2 (3, 7, 11, 13), *k3, p2, k3, p3, k2, p3, k3, p2, k2*, rep from * twice more, k to end.

Row 30 (RS): p3 (4, 8, 12, 14), *p1, [sl 1 to cn and hold to back, k2, p1 from cn], p2, [sl 1 to cn and hold to back, k1, p1 from cn], [sl 2 to cn and hold to front, p1, k2 from cn], [sl 1 to cn and hold to back, k2, p1 from cn], [sl 1 to cn and hold to front, p1, k1 from cn], p2, [sl 2 to cn and hold to front, p1, k2 from cn], p1, MB*, rep from * twice more (but end last rep with p1 instead of MB), p to end.

Row 31 (WS): k2 (3, 7, 11, 13), *k2, p2, k3, p1, k2, p4, k2, p1, k3, p2, k1*, rep from * twice more, k to end.

Row 32 (RS): p3 (4, 8, 12, 14), *p1, k2, p2, [sl 1 to cn and hold to back, k1, p1 from cn], p2, [sl 2 to cn and hold to front, k2, k2 from cn], p2, [sl 1 to cn and hold to front, p1, k1 from cn], p2, k2, p2*, rep from * twice more, p to end.

Row 33 (WS): k2 (3, 7, 11, 13), *k2, p2, k2, p1, k3, p4, k3, p1, k2, p2, k1*, rep from * twice more, k to end.

Row 34 (RS): p3 (4, 8, 12, 14), *p1, k2, p1, [sl 1 to cn and hold to back, k1, p1 from cn], p3, k4, p3, [sl 1 to cn and hold to front, p1, k1 from cn], p1, k2, p2*, rep from * twice more, p to end.

Row 35 (WS): k2 (3, 7, 11, 13), *k2, p2, k1, p1, k4, p4, k4, p1, k1, p2, k1*, rep from * twice more, k to end.

Row 36 (RS): p3 (4, 8, 12, 14), *p1, k2, p1, [sl 1 to cn and hold to front, p1, k1 from cn], p3, [sl 2 to cn and hold to front, k2, k2 from cn], p3, [sl 1 to cn and hold to back, k1, p1 from cn], p1, k2, p2*, rep from * twice more, p to end.

Row 37 (WS): k2 (3, 7, 11, 13), *k2, p2, k2, p1, k3, p4, k3, p1, k2, p2, k1*, rep from * twice more, k to end.

Row 38 (RS): p3 (4, 8, 12, 14), *p1, k2, p2, [sl 1 to cn and hold to front, p1, k1 from cn], p1, [sl 1 to cn and hold to back, k2, p1 from cn], [sl 2 to cn and hold to front, p1, k2 from cn], p1, [sl 1 to cn and hold to back, k1, p1 from cn], p2, k2, p2*, rep from * twice more, p to end.

Row 39 (WS): k2 (3, 7, 11, 13), *k2, p2, k3, p1, k1, p2, k2 p2, k1, p1, k3, p2, k1*, rep from * twice more, k to end.

Row 40 (RS): p3 (4, 8, 12, 14), *p1, k2, p3, [sl 2 to cn and hold to back, k2, k2 from cn], p2, [sl 2 to cn and hold to front, k2, k2 from cn], p3, k2, p2*, rep from * twice more, p to end.

Row 41 (WS): k2 (3, 7, 11, 13), * k2, p2, k3, p2, k1, p1, k2, p1, k1, p2, k3, p2, k1*, rep from * twice more, k to end.

Row 42 (RS): p3 (4, 8, 12, 14), *p1, k2, p2, [sl 1 to cn and hold to back, k2, p1 from cn], p1, [sl 1 to cn and hold to back, k1, p1 from cn], [sl 1 to cn and hold to back, k1, p1 from cn], p1, [sl 2 to cn and hold to front, p1, k2 from cn], p2, k2, p2*, rep from * twice more, p to end.

Row 43 (WS): k2 (3, 7, 11, 13), *[k2, p2] twice, [k3, p2] twice, k2, p2, k1*, rep from * twice more, k to end.

Row 44 (RS): p3 (4, 8, 12, 14), *p1, k2, p2, [k2, p3] twice, [k2, p2] twice*, rep from * twice more, p to end.

Row 45 (WS): rep Row 43.

Row 46 (RS): p3 (4, 8, 12, 14), *p1, k2, p2, [sl 2 to cn and hold to front, p1, k2 from cn], p1, [sl 1 to cn and hold to back, k1, p1 from cn], [sl 1 to cn and hold to front, p1, k1 from cn], p1, [sl 1 to cn and hold to back, k2, p1 from cn], p2, k2, p2*, rep from * twice more, p to end.

Row 47 (WS): rep Row 41.

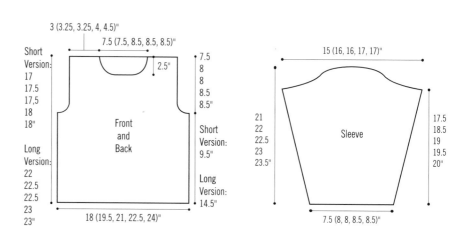

Row 48 (RS): p3 (4, 8, 12, 14), *p1, k2, p3, [sl 2 to cn and hold to front, p1, k2 from cn], p4, [sl 1 to cn and hold to back, k2, p1 from cn], p3, k2, p2*, p to end.

Row 49 (WS): k2 (3, 7, 11, 13), *k2, p2, [k4, p2] 3 times, k1*, rep from * twice more, k to end.

Row 50 (RS): p3 (4, 8, 12, 14), *p1, k2, p4, [sl 2 to cn and hold to front, k1, k2 from cn], p2, [sl 1 to cn and hold to back, k2, k1 from cn], p4, k2, p2*, rep from * twice more, p to end.

Row 51 (WS): k2 (3, 7, 11, 13), *k2, p2, k4, p3, k2, p3, k4, p2, k1*, rep from * twice more, k to end.

Row 52 (RS): p3 (4, 8, 12, 14), *p1, k2, p3, [sl 1 to cn and hold to back, k1, p1 from cn], [sl 2 to cn and hold to front, p1, k2 from cn], [sl 1 to cn and hold to back, k2, p1 from cn], [sl 1 to cn and hold to front, p1, k1 from cn], p3, k2, p2*, rep from * twice more, p to end.

Repeat Rows 31 through 52 to top of Front; AT THE SAME TIME, follow Neck shaping and completion directions as given on page 35.

BACK

Work as for Front, but work even from armhole shaping (omit neck shaping) until length of piece matches length of Front piece to shoulder, then bind off all sts.

SLEEVES

With smaller needles, cast on 38 (40, 40, 42, 42) sts and work seed-stitch band as for Front.

Change to larger needles and work Diamond Cable pat as follows, noting "Sleeve shaping" instructions before proceeding:

CHARTED INSTRUCTIONS

Row 1 (WS): k4 (5, 5, 6, 6), work across Row 1 of Diamond Cable chart, k4 (5, 5, 6, 6).

Row 2 (RS): p4 (5, 5, 6, 6), work across Row 2 of Diamond Cable chart, p4 (5, 5, 6, 6).

Pattern placement is now established. Continue to Row 16 of chart, then rep Rows 1 through 16, and skip to "Sleeve shaping."

WRITTEN INSTRUCTIONS

Row 1 (WS): k4 (5, 5, 6, 6), placing marker on last st, p3, k7, p2, k6, p2, k7, p3; place marker on next st and k4 (5, 5, 6, 6).

Continue in Diamond Cable pat as given for Front, but working directions given for sts between markers only once. Work from Row 2 through Row 16, then rep Rows 1 through 16 of pat.

Sleeve shaping: AT THE SAME TIME, inc 1 at each side every 2nd row 3 times, then every 4th row to 78 (84, 84, 90, 90) sts. Work incs in reverse st st.

Work even, if necessary, until piece measures 17½ (18½, 19, 19½, 20)" from bottom edge, ending with RS facing for next row. Shape sleeve cap by binding off sts at beginning of each row in the following sequence: Bind off 4 (6, 6, 6, 6) sts at each side once; bind off 3 (3, 3, 4, 4) sts at each side 4 times; bind off 2 sts at each side 4 times; bind off 3 sts at each side twice; bind off 4 sts at each side once; bind off all remaining sts.

Pin pieces to measurements as shown and block as directed for gauge swatch.

Sew right shoulder seam.

Collar: using smaller needles and with RS facing you, tie on yarn and pick up 20 (20, 23, 23, 23) sts along Left Front neck edge, 12 sts across bound-off sts at center Front neck edge, 20 (20, 23, 23, 23) sts along Right Front neck edge, and 38 (38, 42, 42, 42) sts along Back neck edge, to 90 (90, 100, 100, 100) sts.

Work seed stitch for 3 rows. Bind off as follows: bind off 1 st knitwise,* bind off 1 picot st (see below), bind off 4 sts*, rep from * to last 3 sts, then bind off 1 picot st, bind off last sts knitwise.

To bind off 1 picot st: purl into the next st 4 times: first in the front of the loop, then the back, then the front again, then the back again, so that the one st now has 4 loops. Then with the point of the left needle, lift the first of the four loops at the right of the right-hand needle over all loops on right-hand needle. Keep lifting the farthest-right loop over the others until you have one loop remaining on right-hand needle.

Sew left shoulder seam and collar seam. Sew sleeve seams and side seams. Set in sleeves to armholes. ❧

gatineau

With its loose oversized fit, the Gatineau design suits just about everyone. The cables cover the sleeve and run up the saddle shoulder extension, tying the sleeves together with the center front cables. Blocks of seed stitch pepper the front and back for added textural interest.

SKILL LEVEL: EXPERIENCED

MEASUREMENTS

SIZES (in inches)	TEENS			ADULTS			
	12	14	16	SM	MD	LG	XL
Finished Chest	32	36	40	44	48	52	56
Finished Length	24	25	26	27	28	29	30

MATERIALS

Yarn: Patons Classic Merino 100% Wool #229 (221 yds or 204 m/100 gr ball). *See also page 126 for yarn information.*

NO. OF BALLS	TEENS			ADULTS			
	12	14	16	SM	MD	LG	XL
#229	6	6	7	8	8	9	9

Needles: 1 pr. each U.S sizes 6 and 7 (4 mm and 4.5 mm) needles OR SIZE TO OBTAIN GAUGE

Stitch markers (you can use loops of contrasting yarn)

Cable needle

SPECIAL ABBREVIATIONS

Back Cross Cable = Sl the next 2 sts to a cable needle and hold to the back of the work, k2, then k the 2 sts from cable needle.

FPC = Front Purl Cross: hold 2 sts to front on cable needle, p1, k2 from cable needle.

BPC = Back Purl Cross: hold 1 st to back on cable needle, k2, p1 from cable needle.

GAUGE

20 sts and 26 rows = 4" in st st using larger needles

To work Gauge Swatch: with larger needles, cast on 24 stitches and work st st (k all sts on RS rows and p all sts on WS rows). Block swatch by laying it flat and applying lots of steam with steam iron held just above the swatch. Let cool and dry. If you have too many sts and rows to the inch, switch to a larger needle; too few means you should use a smaller needle.

Your garment will not fit properly if the tension gauge is incorrect! Take the time to check by making gauge swatch.

Directions are given for Teens' size 12. Teens' sizes 14 and 16, and Adults' sizes Small, Medium, Large, and Extra-Large are given in parentheses. Where there is only one number, it applies to all sizes.

CABLE PANEL (worked over 25 sts)

Rows 1 and 3 (RS): *p1, k1, p1, k2, [p1, k1] twice, k2*, rep from * once more, p1, k1, p1.

Rows 2 and 4 (WS): *p1, k1, p1, p2, [k1, p1] twice, p2*, rep from * once more, p1, k1, p1.

Row 5 (RS): *p3, FPC, p2, BPC*, rep from * once more, p3.

Row 6 (WS): *k4, p2, k2, p2, k1*, rep from * once more, k3.

Row 7 (RS): *p4, FPC, BPC, p1*, rep from * once more, p3.

Row 8 (WS): *k5, p4, k2*, rep from * once more, k3.

Row 9 (RS): *p5, Back Cross Cable, p2*, rep from * once more, p3.

Row 10 (WS): *k5, p4, k2*, rep from * once more, k3.

Row 11 (RS): *p4, BPC, FPC, p1*, rep from * once more, p3.

Row 12 (WS): Rep Row 6.

Row 13 (RS): *p3, BPC, p2, FPC*, rep from * once more, p3.

Row 14 (WS): rep Row 2.

FRONT

With smaller needles, cast on 85 (95, 105, 115, 125, 135, 145) sts and work band as follows:

(RS Rows): k0 (1, 0, 1, 0, 1, 0), *p1, k1*, rep from * 14 (16, 19, 21, 24, 26, 29) times more, work 1st row of Cable Panel, *k1, p1*, rep from * to last 0 (1, 0, 1, 0, 1, 0) st, k0 (1, 0, 1, 0, 1, 0).

(WS Rows): k0 (1, 0, 1, 0, 1, 0), *p1, k1*, rep from * 14 (16, 19, 21, 24, 26, 29) times more, work 2nd row of Cable Panel, *k1, p1*, rep from * to last 0 (1, 0, 1, 0, 1, 0) st, k0 (1, 0, 1, 0, 1, 0).

Rep the last 2 rows twice more.

Change to larger needles and work as follows:

Row 1 (RS): k30 (35, 40, 45, 50, 55, 60), work 5th row of Cable Panel, k to end.

Row 2 (WS): p30 (35, 40, 45, 50, 55, 60), work 6th row of Cable Panel, p to end.

Row 3 (RS): k0 (5, 0, 5, 0, 5, 0), *[p1, k1] twice, p1, k5,* rep from * 2 (2, 3, 3, 4, 4, 5) more times, work 7th row of Cable Panel, *k5, [p1, k1] twice, p1*, rep from * 2 (2, 3, 3, 4, 4, 5) more times, k0 (5, 0, 5, 0, 5, 0).

Row 4 (WS): p0 (5, 0, 5, 0, 5, 0), *[p1, k1] twice, p1, p5*, rep from * 2 (2, 3, 3, 4, 4, 5) more times, work 8th row of Cable Panel, *p5, [p1, k1] twice, p1*, rep from * 2 (2, 3, 3, 4, 4, 5) more times, p0 (5, 0, 5, 0, 5, 0).

Row 5 (RS): k0 (5, 0, 5, 0, 5, 0), *[p1, k1] twice, p1, k5,* rep from * 2 (2, 3, 3, 4, 4, 5) more times, work 9th row of Cable Panel, *k5, [p1, k1] twice, p1*, rep from * 2 (2, 3, 3, 4, 4, 5) more times, k0 (5, 0, 5, 0, 5, 0).

Row 6 (WS): p0 (5, 0, 5, 0, 5, 0), *[p1, k1] twice, p1, p5*, rep from * 2 (2, 3, 3, 4, 4, 5) more times, work 10th row of Cable Panel, *p5, [p1, k1] twice, p1*, rep from * 2 (2, 3, 3, 4, 4, 5) more times, p0 (5, 0, 5, 0, 5, 0).

Row 7 (RS): k0 (5, 0, 5, 0, 5, 0), *[p1, k1] twice, p1, k5,* rep from * 2 (2, 3, 3, 4, 4, 5) more times, work 11th row of Cable Panel, *k5, [p1, k1] twice, p1*, rep from * 2 (2, 3, 3, 4, 4, 5) more times, k0 (5, 0, 5, 0, 5, 0).

Row 8 (WS): p30 (35, 40, 45, 50, 55, 60), work 12th row of Cable Panel, p to end.

Row 9 (RS): k30 (35, 40, 45, 50, 55, 60), work 13th row of Cable Panel, k to end.

Row 10 (WS): *12, 16, MD, and XL:* *p5, k1, [p1, k1] twice*, rep from * 2 (3, 4, 5) more times, work 2nd row of Cable Panel, *k1, [p1, k1] twice, p5*, rep from * 2 (3, 4, 5) more times. *14, SM, and LG:* [k1, p1] twice, k1, *p5, k1 [p1, k1] twice*, rep from * 2 (3, 4) more times, work 2nd row of Cable Panel, *k1, [p1, k1] twice, p5*, rep from * 2 (3, 4) more times, k1, [p1, k1] twice.

Row 11 (RS):*12, 16, MD, and XL:* *k6, [p1, k1] twice*, rep from * 2 (3, 4, 5) more times, work 1st row of Cable Panel, *[k1, p1] twice, k6*, rep from * 2 (3, 4, 5) more times. *14, SM, and LG:* [k1, p1] twice, k1, *k6, [p1, k1] twice*, rep from * 2 (3, 4) more times, work 1st row of Cable Panel, * [k1, p1] twice, k6*, rep from * 2 (3, 4) more times, [k1, p1] twice, k1.

Row 12 (WS): Rep Row 10.

Row 13 (RS): *12, 16, MD, and XL:* *k6, [p1, k1] twice*, rep from * 2 (3, 4, 5) more times, work 3rd row of Cable Panel, *[k1, p1] twice, k6*, rep from * 2 (3, 4, 5) more times. *14, SM, and LG:* [k1, p1] twice, k1, *k6, [p1, k1] twice*, rep from * 2 (3, 4) more times, work 3rd row of Cable Panel, *[k1, p1] twice, k6*, rep from * 2 (3, 4) more times, [k1, p1] twice, k1.

Row 14 (WS): Rep Row 10.

These last 14 rows form pat.

Rep the last 14 rows until piece measures 16 (16½, 17½, 18, 18½, 19, 19½)" from bottom edge, ending with RS facing for next row.

Armhole shaping (RS): bind off 10 sts at beginning of next 2 rows, then work in pat to end. You should now have 65 (75, 85, 95, 105, 115, 125) sts remaining.

Left neck shaping (RS): work 33 (38, 43, 48, 53, 58, 63) sts in pat. Leave remaining sts on spare needle. Turn.

Next row (WS): Work 1 row in pat.

Next row (RS): Work in pat to last 16 sts, k2tog, k1, work in pat to end. Rep the last 2 rows 7 (8, 8, 9, 9, 9, 9) more times.

Work 3 rows in pat.

Next row (RS): work in pat to last 16 sts, k2tog, k1, work in pat to end. Rep the last 4 rows 1 (2, 2, 5, 5, 5, 5) more times. You should now have 23 (26, 31, 32, 37, 42, 47) sts remaining.

Work even, if necessary, until piece measures 22 (23, 24, 25, 26, 27, 28)" from bottom edge, ending with RS facing for next row.

Bind off all but last 16 sts, then work in pat to end.

Neckline extension: keeping in pat, work the remaining 16 sts until extension measures 7 (7, 7, 8, 8, 8, 8)" from shoulder bind offs. Bind off all remaining sts.

Right neck shaping: with RS facing, join yarn and cast on 1 st at beginning of row. Work 1st 13 sts (including cast-on st) in cable pat as established, k1, sl 1, k1, psso, work in pat to end.

Next row (WS): work 1 row in pat. Rep the last 2 rows 7 (8, 8, 9, 9, 9, 9) more times.

Work 2 rows in pat.

Next row (RS): Work 1st 13 sts in cable pat, k1, sl 1, k1, psso, work in pat to end.

Next row (WS): work 1 row in pat. Rep the last 4 rows 1 (2, 2, 5, 5, 5, 5) more times. You should now have 23 (26, 31, 32, 37, 42, 47) sts remaining.

Work even, if necessary, until piece measures 22 (23, 24, 25, 26, 27, 28)" from bottom edge, ending with WS facing for next row.

Bind off all but last 16 sts, then work in pat to end.

Neckline extension: keeping in pat, work the remaining 16 sts until extension measures 7 (7, 7, 8, 8, 8, 8)" from shoulder bind offs. Bind off all remaining sts.

BACK

With smaller needles, cast on 85 (95, 105, 115, 125, 135, 145) sts and work 6 rows of seed-stitch band as follows: k1, *p1, k1*, rep from * to end.

Change to larger needles and work as follows:

Row 1 (RS): knit.

Row 2 (WS): purl.

Row 3 (RS): k0 (5, 0, 5, 0, 5, 0), *[p1, k1] twice, p1, k5*, rep from * to last 5 (10, 5, 10, 5, 10, 5) sts, [p1, k1] twice, p1, k0 (5, 0, 5, 0, 5, 0).

Row 4 (WS): p0 (5, 0, 5, 0, 5, 0), *[p1, k1] twice, p6*, rep from * to last 5 (10, 5, 10, 5, 10, 5) sts, [p1, k1] twice, p1, p0 (5, 0, 5, 0, 5, 0).

Row 5 (RS): rep Row 3.

Row 6 (WS): rep Row 4.

Row 7 (RS): rep Row 3.

Row 8 (WS): purl.

Row 9 (RS): knit.

Row 10 (WS): *12, 16, MD, and XL:* *p5, [k1, p1] twice, k1*, rep from * to last 5 sts, p5. *14, SM, and LG:* [k1, p1] twice, k1, *p5, [k1, p1] twice, k1*, rep from * to end.

Row 11 (RS): *12, 16, MD, and XL:* *k6, [p1, k1] twice*, rep from * to last 5 sts, end k5. *14, SM and LG:* [k1, p1] twice, k1, *k6, [p1, k1] twice*, rep from * to end.

Row 12 (WS): rep Row 10.

Row 13 (RS): rep Row 11.

Row 14 (WS): rep Row 10.

These last 14 rows form pat.

Rep the last 14 rows until piece measures 16 (16½, 17½, 18, 18½, 19, 19½)" from bottom edge, ending with RS facing for next row.

Armhole shaping (RS): bind off 10 sts at beginning of next 2 rows, then work in pat to end. You should now have 65 (75, 85, 95, 105, 115, 125) sts remaining.

Continue in pat until piece measures 22 (23, 24, 25, 26, 27, 28)" from bottom edge, ending with RS facing for next row. Bind off.

SLEEVES

Note: read through sleeve directions before proceeding.

With smaller needles, cast on 47 sts. Establish Cable Panel placement as follows; AT THE SAME TIME, inc 1 at each side on 3rd row, then every 2nd row 1 (1, 1, 2, 2, 4, 4) times, then every 4th row thereafter. Work your incs into cable pat until you have 69 (91, 91, 91, 113, 113, 113) sts, then work any remaining incs in seed stitch.

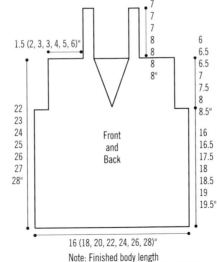

1.5 (2, 3, 3, 4, 5, 6)"

7
7
7
8
8
8
8"

6
6.5
6.5
7
7.5
8
8.5"
16
16.5
17.5
18
18.5
19
19.5"

22
23
24
25
26
27
28"

Front and Back

16 (18, 20, 22, 24, 26, 28)"

Note: Finished body length incl. saddle shoulder = 24 (25, 26, 27, 28, 29, 30)"

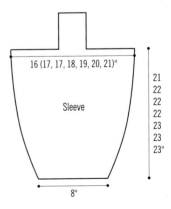

16 (17, 17, 18, 19, 20, 21)"

Sleeve

21
22
22
22
23
23
23"

8"

Rows 1 and 3 (RS): *p1, k1, p1, k2, [p1, k1] twice, k2*, rep from * to last 3 sts, p1, k1, p1.

Rows 2 and 4 (WS): *p1, k1, p1, p2, [k1, p1] twice, p2*, rep from * to last 3 sts, p1, k1, p1.

Row 5 (RS): *p3, FPC, p2, BPC*, rep from * to last 3 sts, p3.

Row 6 (WS): *k4, p2, k2, p2, k1*, rep from * to last 3 sts, k3. Change to larger needles.

Row 7 (RS): *p4, FPC, BPC, p1*, rep from * to last 3 sts, p3.

Row 8 (WS): *k5, p4, k2*, rep from * to last 3 sts, k3.

Row 9 (RS): *p5, Back Cross Cable, p2*, rep from * to last 3 sts, p3.

Row 10 (WS): Rep Row 8.

Row 11 (RS): *p4, BPC, FPC, p1*, rep from * to last 3 sts, p3.

Row 12 (WS): rep Row 6.

Row 13 (RS): *p3, BPC, p2, FPC*, rep from * to last 3 sts, p3.

Row 14 (WS): rep Row 2.

These 14 rows form pat.

Rep the last 14 rows (using larger needles), making incs at sides as directed above, until you have 89 (95, 101, 107, 113, 119, 125) sts, then work even in pat as established until piece measures 21 (22, 22, 22, 23, 23, 23)" from bottom edge, ending with RS facing for next row.

Continuing in pat, bind off 32 (35, 38, 41, 44, 47, 50) sts at beginning of next 2 rows, leaving 25 sts remaining for saddle shoulder extension.

Saddle shoulder extension: Continue in pat as established on remaining 25 sts until length of piece measured from bound-off sts measures 1½ (2, 3, 3, 4, 5, 6)". Bind off.

FINISHING

Pin pieces to measurements as shown and block as directed for Gauge Swatch.

Neck edge finishing: with right side of work facing and smaller needles, pick up 46 (50, 50, 60, 62, 64, 66) sts from end of extension to center front V-neck, and 46 (50, 50, 60, 62, 64, 66) sts from point of center front V-neck to end of other extension. Knit one row, and k2tog at V-neck point to define point of V. Bind off all sts knitwise.

Following Sewing Diagram shown below, sew saddle shoulder extensions to Front and Back shoulders, and sew tops of sleeves to armholes. Sew short neckline extension seams together and, placing seam at center back neck edge, sew to back neck edge. Sew upper sleeve seams to armhole bound-off sts. Sew side seams and sleeve seams. 🍁

SEWING DIAGRAM

Back

Sleeve   Sleeve

Front

twister

A diagonal rib adds rich surface texture and a sense of movement to this funnel-necked pullover. Sized for both teens and women, this simple twist-stitch pattern knits up quickly with minimal shaping.

MEASUREMENTS

SIZES (in inches)	TEENS			WOMEN			
	12	14	16	SM	MD	LG	XL
Finished Bust	34	36	39	40	43	46	48
Finished Length	21	22	22	23	23	24	24

MATERIALS

Yarn: Patons Classic Merino 100% Wool #207 (221 yds or 204 m/100 gr ball). *See also page 126 for yarn information.*

NO. OF BALLS	TEENS			WOMEN			
	12	14	16	SM	MD	LG	XL
#207	5	5	5	6	6	7	7

Needles: 1 pr. U.S. size 7 (4.5 mm) needles OR SIZE TO OBTAIN GAUGE.

SPECIAL ABBREVIATIONS

The following twist stitches reverse the order in which the next 2 stitches are knit, forming a twisted effect.

RT = Right Twist: with the yarn in back, ignore the next st on left needle and k the 2nd st through front of loop, do not slide off left needle, then p the 1st st (the previously ignored st) through back of loop, slip both sts from needle.

LT = Left Twist: with the yarn in back, ignore the next st on left needle and k the 2nd st through back of loop, do not slide off left needle, bring the right needle around to front of knitting and k the 1st st (the previously ignored st) through front of loop, slip both sts from needle.

GAUGE

23 sts and 26 rows = 4" in pattern

To work Gauge Swatch: cast on 27 sts and work Twist Stitch pattern (multiple of 4 sts plus 3) as follows:

Row 1 (WS): k3, *p1, k3*, rep from * to end.

Row 2 (RS): *p2, RT*, rep from * to last 3 sts, p2, k1.

Row 3 (WS): *p1, k3*, rep from * to last 3 sts, p1, k2.

Row 4 (RS): p1, *RT, p2*, rep from * to last 2 sts, RT.

Row 5 (WS): k1, *p1, k3*, rep from * to last 2 sts, p1, k1.

Row 6 (RS): *RT, p2*, rep from * to last 3 sts, RT, p1.

Row 7 (WS): k2, *p1, k3*, rep from * to last st, k1.

Row 8 (RS): p3, *RT, p2*, rep from * to end.

These 8 rows form pat.

Rep the last 8 rows until swatch measures 4" from bottom edge. Bind off all sts in pat. Block swatch by laying it flat and applying lots of steam with steam iron held just above the swatch. Let cool and dry. If you have too many sts and rows to the inch, switch to a larger needle; if you have too few, use a smaller needle.

Your garment will not fit properly if the tension gauge is incorrect! Take time to check by making gauge swatch.

Directions are given for Teens' size 12. Teens' sizes 14 and 16, and Womens' sizes Small, Medium, Large, and Extra-Large are given in parentheses. Where there is only one number, it applies to all sizes.

BACK

Cast on 99 (103, 111, 115, 123, 131, 139) sts and work three rows for beginning as follows:

(RS): p3, *k1, p3*, rep from * to end.

(WS): k3, *p1, k3*, rep from * to end.

(RS): p3, *k1, p3*, rep from * to end.

Begin working pat as for Gauge Swatch, repeating Rows 1 through 8.

When length of piece measures 13 (13½, 13½, 14, 14, 14½, 14½)" from bottom edge, work armhole shaping as follows, keeping in pat as established: Bind off first 3 sts at each side twice, then bind off first 2 sts at each side three times, then bind off first st at each side until you have bound off a total of 16 sts at each armhole. You should now have 67 (71, 79, 83, 91, 99, 107) sts remaining.

Work even in pat as established, until piece measures 21 (22, 22, 23, 23, 24, 24)" from bottom edge, ending with RS facing for next row.

Next Row (RS): bind off all sts in pat (bind off knit sts knitwise and bind off purl sts purlwise).

FRONT

Work exactly as for Back, including armhole shaping, until piece measures 19 (20, 20, 21, 21, 22, 22)" from bottom edge, ending with RS facing for next row.

Neck shaping: work across 28 (30, 34, 36, 40, 44, 48) sts in pat as established, join second ball of yarn, and with second ball, bind off 11 sts and work in pat to end.

Working both sides of neckline at same time with separate balls of yarn, bind off sts at neck edge in the following sequence: Bind off 6 sts at each side of neck edge once; bind off 4 (4, 5, 5, 5, 5, 5) sts at each side of neck edge once; bind off 3 (3, 4, 4, 4, 5, 5) sts at each side of neck edge once; bind off 2 sts at each side of neck edge once; bind off 1 st at each side of neck edge until you have 11 (13, 15, 17, 21, 24, 28) sts remaining at each shoulder.

Work even, if necessary, until piece measures 21 (22, 22, 23, 23, 24, 24)" from bottom edge, ending with RS facing for next row. Bind off all sts in pat.

SLEEVES

Cast on 39 (39, 39, 39, 39, 43, 43) sts and work the 3 beginning rows as for Back.

Begin working pat as given for Gauge Swatch; AT THE SAME TIME, work 1 inc at each side every 4th row until you have a total of 83 (87, 87, 91, 91, 99, 99) sts, working your incs into pat as established. Work even, if necessary, until piece measures 16½ (17½, 18, 18½, 19, 20, 20)" from bottom edge, ending with RS facing for next row.

Cap shaping: continuing in pat, bind off sts in pat at beginning of each row as follows: bind off 4 sts at each side three times, bind off 3 sts at each side 2 (2, 2, 3, 3, 3, 3) times; bind off 1 (1, 1, 2, 2, 2, 2) sts at each side once; bind off 3 sts at each side once; bind off 4 sts at each side once; bind off all remaining sts.

FINISHING

Block pieces to measurements. Sew right shoulder seam.

Collar: with RS facing you, pick up 26 (26, 27, 27, 27, 28, 28) sts along left Front neck edge, pick up 26 (26, 27, 27, 27, 28, 28) sts along right Front neck edge, and pick up 43 (43, 45, 45, 45, 47, 47) sts along Back neck edge, for a total of 95 (95, 99, 99, 99, 103, 103) sts. Work collar as follows:

Row 1 (WS): k3, *p1, k3*, rep from * to end.

Row 2 (RS): p3, *LT, p2*, rep from * to end.

Row 3 (WS): k2, *p1, k3*, rep from * to last st, p1.

Row 4 (RS): *LT, p2*, rep from * to last 3 sts, LT, p1.

Row 5 (WS): k1, *p1, k3*, rep from * to last 2 sts, p1, k1.

Row 6 (RS): p1, *LT, p2*, rep from * to last 2 sts, LT.

Row 7 (WS): *p1, k3*, rep from * to last 3 sts, p1, k2.

Row 8 (RS): p2, *LT, p2*, rep from * to last st, p1.

Rep the last eight rows until collar measures 4½" deep from beginning, ending with RS facing for next row. Bind off all sts in pat.

Sew collar seam and left shoulder seam. Sew sleeve seams and side seams, and set sleeves into armholes. ❦

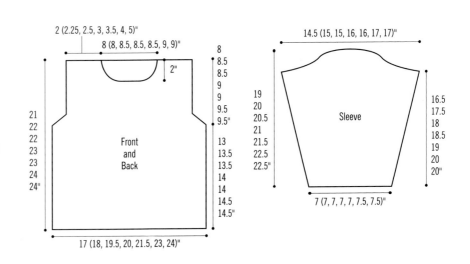

2 (2.25, 2.5, 3, 3.5, 4, 5)"
8 (8, 8.5, 8.5, 8.5, 9, 9)"
2"
8
8.5
8.5
9
9
9.5
9.5"
21
22
22
23
23
24
24"
Front and Back
13
13.5
13.5
14
14
14.5
14.5"
17 (18, 19.5, 20, 21.5, 23, 24)"

14.5 (15, 15, 16, 16, 17, 17)"
19
20
20.5
21
21.5
22.5
22.5"
Sleeve
16.5
17.5
18
18.5
19
20
20"
7 (7, 7, 7, 7, 7.5, 7.5)"

winter

wishbone

Cable patterns usually follow certain conventions: the cables line up in nice, neat vertical columns with purl stitches in between. But what if they're staggered, and piled together without any purl stitches? The result is an intriguing, not-quite-random texture, shown in sharp relief in a chunky gauge, with the added benefit that most of the rows of this pattern are plain stockinette stitch for easy knitting.

SKILL LEVEL: EASY/INTERMEDIATE

MEASUREMENTS

SIZES (in inches)	TEENS			ADULTS			
	12	14	16	SM	MD	LG	XL
Finished Chest	37	39	42	43½	46½	51	52½
Finished Length	22	23½	24½	25½	26½	27	27½

MATERIALS

Yarn: Patons Country Garden DK 100% Wool (127 yds or 117 m/50 gr ball). *See also page 126 for yarn information.*

NO. OF BALLS	TEENS			ADULTS			
	12	14	16	SM	MD	LG	XL
Color #73	22	24	28				
Color #79				30	32	34	36

Please see Table of Contents for photo of teens version.

Needles: 1 pr. each U.S. sizes 7 and 9 (4.5 mm and 5.5 mm) needles OR SIZE TO OBTAIN GAUGE

Large cable needle

Spare needle or stitch holder

SPECIAL ABBREVIATIONS

C6F = slip 3 sts to cable needle and hold to front, k3, k3 from cable needle.

C6B = slip 3 sts to cable needle and hold to back, k3, k3 from cable needle.

GAUGE

21 sts = 4" wide in pattern using larger needles and 2 strands of yarn

To work Gauge Swatch: with larger needles and holding 2 strands of yarn together, cast on 26 sts and work wishbone cable pat as given below, for smallest size of Front, until piece measures 4" from bottom edge. Bind off. Block swatch by laying flat and applying lots of steam with steam iron held just above the swatch. Let cool and dry. If you have too many sts to the inch, switch to a larger needle; too few means you should use a smaller needle.

Your garment will not fit properly if the tension gauge is incorrect! Take the time to check by making gauge swatch.

Directions are given for Teens' size 12. Teens' sizes 14, 16, and Adults' sizes Small, Medium, Large, and Extra-Large are given in parentheses. Where there is only one number, it applies to all sizes.

FRONT

With smaller needles and holding 2 strands of yarn together, cast on 66 (70, 74, 78, 82, 90, 94) sts.

Work garter st (k all sts on all rows) for 3 rows.

Next row (WS): k1 (3, 1, 3, 1, 1, 3), *inc 1, k1*, rep to last 1 (3, 1, 3, 1, 1, 3) st(s), k1 (3, 1, 3, 1, 1, 3). You should now have 98 (102, 110, 114, 122, 134, 138) sts.

Change to larger needles and work Wishbone Cable pat as follows:

Rows 1 and 5 (RS): knit.

Row 2 and all WS rows: purl.

Row 3 (RS): k1 (3, 1, 3, 1, 1, 3), *C6B, C6F, k12*, rep from * to last 1 (3, 13, 15, 1, 13, 15) st(s). [Sizes 12, 14, MD: k to end.] [Sizes 16, SM, LG, XL: C6B, C6F, k to end.]

Row 7 (RS): k1 (3, 1, 3, 1, 1, 3), *k12, C6B, C6F*, rep from * to last 1 (3, 13, 15, 1, 13, 15) st(s), k to end.

Row 8 (WS): purl.

Rep these 8 rows until piece measures as close as possible to 14 (15, 15¼, 16, 16, 16¼, 16)" from bottom edge, while ending with Row 2 or Row 6 of pattern.

Armhole shaping: at beginning of next 2 rows, bind off 12 (14, 12, 14, 12, 12, 14) sts, work to end in pat. You should now have 74 (74, 86, 86, 98, 110, 110) sts remaining.

Continue working pat until piece measures as close as possible to 6 (6½, 7¼, 7½, 8½, 8¾, 9½)" from armhole shaping, while ending with Row 2 or Row 6 of pattern.

Left side neck shaping (RS): work 31 (31, 37, 37, 43, 49, 49) sts in pat. Turn, leaving remaining sts on spare needle.

Next row (WS): bind off 3 (3, 5, 5, 5, 6, 6) sts, purl to end.

Next row (RS): work in pat to last 2 sts, k2tog.

Next row (WS): bind off 2 sts, purl to end. Rep the last 2 rows once more.

Next row (RS): work in pat to last 2 sts, k2tog.

Next row (WS): bind off 1 st, purl to end. Rep the last 2 rows until you have 18 (18, 22, 22, 26, 31, 31) sts remaining for shoulder. Work even (no shaping), if necessary, until piece measures 8 (8½, 9¼, 9½, 10½, 10¾, 11½)" from armhole shaping, while ending with Row 2 or Row 6 of pattern. Bind off.

Right side neck shaping (RS): join doubled yarn to first st and bind off 12 sts, work pat to end.

Next row (WS): p to last 2 sts, p2tog.

Next row (RS): bind off 3 (3, 5, 5, 5, 6, 6) sts, work pat to end.

Next row (WS): p to last 2 sts, p2tog.

Next row (RS): bind off 2 sts, work pat to end. Rep the last 2 rows once more.

Next row (WS): purl to last 2 sts, p2tog.

Next row (RS): bind off 1 st, work pat to end. Rep the last 2 rows until you have 18 (18, 22, 22, 26, 31, 31) sts remaining for shoulder. Work even (no shaping), if necessary, until piece measures as close as possible to 8 (8½, 9¼, 9½, 10½, 10¾, 11½)" from armhole shaping, while ending with Row 2 or Row 6 of pattern. Bind off.

BACK

Work as for Front, up to "Left side neck shaping." Work even in pat until piece matches length of Front to bottom edge, ending with RS facing for next row.

Bind off 18 (18, 22, 22, 26, 31, 31) sts at beginning of each of the next 2 rows. Leave remaining 38 (38, 42, 42, 46, 48, 48) sts for Back neck on spare needle or holder.

SLEEVES

With smaller needles and holding 2 strands of yarn together, cast on 31 (33, 37, 39, 43, 45, 49) sts.

Work garter st (k all sts on all rows) for 3 rows.

Next row (WS): inc 1 on every st across row. You should now have 62 (66, 74, 78, 86, 90, 98) sts.

Change to larger needles and work Wishbone Cable pat as follows:

Rows 1 and 5 (RS): knit.

Row 2 and all WS rows: purl.

Row 3 (RS): k1 (3, 1, 3, 1, 3, 1), *C6B, C6F, k12*, rep from * to last 13 (15, 1, 3, 13, 15, 1) st(s). [Sizes 12, 14, MD, LG: C6B, C6F, k to end.] [Sizes 16, SM, XL: k to end.]

Row 7 (RS): k1 (3, 1, 3, 1, 3, 1), *k12, C6B, C6F*, rep from * to last 13 (15, 1, 3, 13, 15, 1) st(s), k to end.

Row 8 (WS): purl.

Rep the last 8 rows; AT THE SAME TIME, inc 1 st at each side every 10th (10th, 10th, 12th, 12th, 12th, 12th) row, working your incs in pat until you have a total of 86 (90, 98, 102, 110, 114, 122) sts.

Work even (no incs) until piece measures as close as possible to 20 (22, 22, 23, 23, 23, 24)" from bottom edge, while ending with Row 2 or Row 6 of pattern. Bind off.

FINISHING

Sew right shoulder seam.

Collar: with RS facing, using smaller needles and holding 2 strands of yarn together, pick up and knit 24 (24, 25, 25, 27, 27, 28) sts along left Front neck edge, pick up and knit 24 (24, 25, 25, 27, 27, 28) sts along right Front neck edge, knit across 38 (38, 42, 42, 46, 48, 48) sts from Back neck st holder and dec 3 sts evenly across these sts. You should have a total of 83 (83, 89, 89, 97, 99, 101) sts for collar. Work 4 rows garter st. Bind off.

Sew left shoulder seam and collar seam. Sew sleeve top to vertical armhole edges. Sew upper section of sleeve underarm seam to armhole bound-off sts. Sew side seams and remaining sleeve seams together. ✤

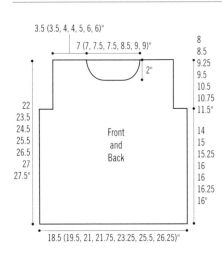

3.5 (3.5, 4, 4, 5, 6, 6)"

7 (7, 7.5, 7.5, 8.5, 9, 9)"

2"

8
8.5
9.25
9.5
10.5
10.75
11.5"

22
23.5
24.5
25.5
26.5
27
27.5"

Front
and
Back

14
15
15.25
16
16
16.25
16"

18.5 (19.5, 21, 21.75, 23.25, 25.5, 26.25)"

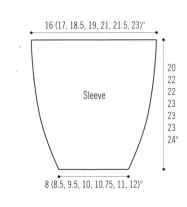

16 (17, 18.5, 19, 21, 21.5, 23)"

Sleeve

20
22
22
23
23
23
24"

8 (8.5, 9.5, 10, 10.75, 11, 12)"

kells twinset

Celtic art and manuscripts inspire designers in every field – for knitters, those rhythmic interlocking borders translate beautifully into cable stitchwork. I also echoed the looping, twisting look of Celtic calligraphy with an interesting button closure, making the button loops flow uninterrupted from the cable pattern. The matching high-necked shell is a simpler piece that picks up the unique rib treatment from the cardigan.

CARDIGAN SKILL LEVEL: EXPERIENCED, SHELL SKILL LEVEL: VERY EASY

MEASUREMENTS

SIZES (in inches)	TEENS		WOMEN			
	12	14	SM	MD	LG	XL
Cardigan Finished Bust	32½	33½	42½	43½	52¾	54½
Cardigan Finished Length	29	29	29½	29½	30½	30½
Shell Finished Bust	27	31	35	39	43	47
Shell Finished Length	20	20½	21	21½	22	22½

MATERIALS

Yarn: Patons Country Garden DK 100% Wool #58 (127 yds or 117 m/50 gr ball). *See also page 126 for yarn information.*

NO. OF BALLS	TEENS		WOMEN			
	12	14	SM	MD	LG	XL
Cardigan	14	15	17	18	20	21
Shell	5	6	6	7	7	8

Needles: 1 pr. U.S. size 6 (4 mm) needles OR SIZE TO FIT GAUGE

Cable needle for cardigan

Spare needle or stitch holder

Three 1½" shank buttons and three ½" sew-through buttons for cardigan

2 safety pins

SPECIAL ABBREVIATIONS

M1 purlwise = make one increase by lifting strand between last-worked and next st onto left needle and purling into the back of this loop.

C6F = sl 3 sts to cable needle and hold to front of work, k3, k3 from cable needle.

C6B = sl 3 sts to cable needle and hold to back of work, k3, k3 from cable needle.

GAUGE

22 sts and 31 rows = 4" in st st

To work Gauge Swatch: cast on 24 sts and work st st (k all sts on RS and p all sts on WS) and work until piece measures 5" from bottom edge. Bind off. Block swatch by laying flat and applying lots of steam with steam iron held just above the swatch. Let cool and dry. If you have too many sts and rows to the inch, switch to a larger needle; too few means you should use a smaller needle.

Your garment will not fit properly if the tension gauge is incorrect! Take the time to check by making gauge swatch.

Directions are given for Teens' size 12. Teens' size 14, and Women's sizes Small, Medium, Large, and Extra-Large are given in parentheses. (Note that due to the large size of pattern repeat, no size 16 is given for this pattern.) Where there is only one number, it applies to all sizes.

CARDIGAN

BRAID CABLE PANEL

(worked over 9 sts)

Row 1 (RS): C6F, k3.

Row 2, 4, and 6 (WS): purl.

Rows 3 and 7 (RS): k9.

Row 5 (RS): k3, C6B.

Row 8 (WS): purl.

These 8 rows form Braid Cable panel.

MAIN PATTERN PANEL

(repeat of 18 sts plus 15 sts)

Row 1 (RS): *[k3, p3] twice, C6F*, rep from * as many times as directed, [k3, p3] twice, k3.

Rows 2, 4, 6, 8, 10, 12, and 14 (WS): [p3, k3] twice, p3, *p6, [k3, p3] twice*, rep from * as many times as directed.

Row 3 (RS): *[k3, p3] twice, k6*, rep from * as many times as directed, [k3, p3] twice, k3.

Row 5 (RS): [k3, p3] twice, k3, *C6B, [p3, k3] twice*, rep from * as many times as directed.

Row 7 (RS): k3 (or "Make loop" as directed for Right Front on page 56) [p3, k3] twice, *k6, [p3, k3] twice*, rep from * as many times as directed.

Rows 9 through 13 (RS): rep Rows 1 through 5.

Row 15 (RS): M1 purlwise, k2, sl 1, k1, psso, p2, k3, p2, k2tog, k2, M1 purlwise, *k3, M1 purlwise, k2, sl 1, k1, psso, p2, k3, p2, k2tog, k2, M1 purlwise*, rep from * as many times as directed.

Row 16 (WS): p4, k2, p3, k2, p4, *yo, p3, pass yo over last 3 sts, p4, k2, p3, k2 , p4*, rep from * as many times as directed.

Row 17 (RS): p1, M1 purlwise, k2, sl 1, k1, psso, p1, k3, p1, k2tog, k2, M1 purlwise, p1, *k3, p1, M1 purlwise, k2, sl 1, k1, psso, p1, k3, p1, k2tog, k2, M1 purlwise, p1*, rep from * as many times as directed.

Row 18 (WS): p5, k1, p3, k1, p5, *yo, p3, pass yo over last 3 sts, p5, k1, p3, k1, p5*, rep from * as many times as directed.

Row 19 (RS): p2, M1 purlwise, k2, sl 1, k1, psso, k3, k2tog, k2, M1 purlwise, p2, *k3, p2, M1 purlwise, k2, sl 1, k1, psso, k3, k2tog, k2, M1 purlwise, p2,*, rep from * as many times as directed.

Rows 20, 22, 24, 26, and 28 (WS): p15, *yo, p3, pass yo over last 3 sts, p15*, rep from * as many times as directed.

Row 21 (RS): p3, C6F, k3, p3, *k3, p3, C6F, k3, p3*, rep from * as many times as directed.

Row 23 (RS): p3, k9, p3, *k3, p3, k9, p3*, rep from * as many times as directed.

Row 25 (RS): p3, k3, C6B, p3, *k3, p3, k3, C6B, p3*, rep from * as many times as directed.

Row 27 (RS): rep Row 23.

Rows 29 through 34: rep Rows 21 through 26.

Row 35 (RS): p2, k2tog, k2, M1 purlwise, k3, M1 purlwise, k2, sl 1, k1, psso, p2, *k3, p2, k2tog, k2, M1 purlwise, k3, M1 purlwise, k2, sl 1, k1, psso, p2*, rep from * as many times as directed.

Row 36 (WS): rep Row 18.

Row 37 (RS): p1, k2tog, k2, M1 purlwise, p1, k3, p1, M1 purlwise, k2, sl 1, k1, psso, p1, *k3, p1, k2tog, k2, M1 purlwise, p1, k3, p1, M1 purlwise, k2, sl 1, k1, psso, p1*, rep from * as many times as directed.

Row 38 (WS): rep Row 16.

Row 39 (RS): k2tog, k2, M1 purlwise, p2, k3, p2, M1 purlwise, k2, sl 1, k1, psso, *k3, k2tog, k2, M1 purlwise, p2, k3, p2, M1 purlwise, k2, sl 1, k1, psso*, rep from * as many times as directed.

Row 40 (WS): rep Row 14.

These 40 rows form Main Pattern panel.

CARDIGAN RIGHT FRONT

Cast on 51 (53, 69, 71, 87, 89) sts.

Work ribbing pat as follows:

RS rows: p1, *p3, k3*, rep from * to last 2 (4, 2, 4, 2, 4) sts, p to end.

WS rows: p14 (16, 14, 16, 14, 16), *yo, p3, pass yo over last 3 sts, p15*, rep from * to last st, p1.

Rep the last 2 rows until piece measures 8½" from bottom edge, ending with RS facing for next row.

Begin braided cable pat as follows:

Row 1 (RS): p4, *C6F, [k3, p3] twice*, rep from * to last 11 (13, 11, 13, 11, 13) sts, C6F, k3, p2 (4, 2, 4, 2, 4).

Rows 2, 4, and 6 (WS): p14 (16, 14, 16, 14, 16), *yo, p3, pass yo over last 3 sts, p15*, rep from * to last st, p1.

Rows 3 and 7 (RS): p4, *k9, p3, k3, p3*, rep from * to last 11 (13, 11, 13, 11, 13) sts, k9, p2 (4, 2, 4, 2, 4).

Row 5 (RS): p4, *k3, C6B, p3, k3, p3*, rep from * to last 11 (13, 11, 13, 11, 13) sts, k3, C6B, p2 (4, 2, 4, 2, 4).

Row 8 (WS): rep Row 2.

Rep Rows 1 through 6 once more.

Work the following 6 prep rows to set up the correct number of sts before beginning Main Pattern, noting that 2 sts are increased on each RS row:

Prep Row 1 (RS): p4, k3, *M1 purlwise, k3, M1 purlwise, k2, sl 1, k1, psso, p2, k3, p2, k2tog, k2*, rep from * 1 (1, 2, 2, 3, 3) time(s) more, [M1 purlwise, k3] twice, p2 (4, 2, 4, 2, 4).

Prep Row 2 (WS): p2 (4, 2, 4, 2, 4), *[p3, k1] twice, p5, yo, p3, pass yo over last 3 sts, p2*, rep from * 1 (1, 2, 2, 3, 3) time(s) more, [p3, k1] twice, p7.

Prep Row 3 (RS): p4, k3, *M1 purlwise, p1, k3, p1, M1 purlwise, k2, sl 1, k1, psso, p1, k3, p1, k2tog, k2*, rep from * 1 (1, 2, 2, 3, 3) time(s) more, M1 purlwise, p1, k3, p1, M1 purlwise, k3, p2 (4, 2, 4, 2, 4).

Prep Row 4 (WS): p2 (4, 2, 4, 2, 4), *[p3, k2] twice, p4, yo, p3, pass yo over last 3 sts, p1*, rep from * 1 (1, 2, 2, 3, 3) time(s) more, [p3, k2] twice, p7.

Prep Row 5 (RS): p4, k3, *M1 purlwise, p2, k3, p2, M1 purlwise, k2, sl 1, k1, psso, k3, k2tog, k2*, rep from * 1 (1, 2, 2, 3, 3) time(s) more, M1 purlwise, p2, k3, p2, M1 purlwise, k3, p2 (4, 2, 4, 2, 4).

Prep Row 6 (WS): p2 (4, 2, 4, 2, 4), *[p3, k3] twice, p6*, rep from * 1 (1, 2, 2, 3, 3) time(s) more, [p3, k3] twice, p7.

You should now have 57 (59, 75, 77, 93, 95) sts.

Begin Main Pattern, working from either charted or written instructions as follows:

CHARTED INSTRUCTIONS

Row 1 (RS): p4, work Row 1 of Main Pattern chart on page 57, working 18-st rep 2 (2, 3, 3, 4, 4) times total, p2 (4, 2, 4, 2, 4).

Row 2 (WS): p2 (4, 2, 4, 2, 4), work Row 2 of Main Pattern chart, working 18-st rep 2 (2, 3, 3, 4, 4) times total, p4.

WRITTEN INSTRUCTIONS

Row 1 (RS): p4, work Row 1 of Main Pattern panel on page 55, repeating written directions between *...* 2 (2, 3, 3, 4, 4) times total, p2 (4, 2, 4, 2, 4).

Row 2 (WS): p2 (4, 2, 4, 2, 4), work Row 2 of Main Pattern panel, repeating written directions between *...* 2 (2, 3, 3, 4, 4) times total, p4.

Main Pattern is now in position. Continue working through remaining rows of Main Pattern, with purl sts at beginning and end of each row as noted in Rows 1 and 2, above. Note that you will work a button loop on the first 3 sts of Row 7 as follows:

Make loop: inc 1, k1, inc 1. Turn, leaving remaining sts for Front on needle until loop is complete. With a spare needle in your right hand, purl these 5 sts. Turn, and knit these 5 sts back onto original needle. Cont working these 5 sts in st st until loop is 4" long, ending with a purl row so that sts are on spare needle. Form a loop, being careful not to twist the sts. Slip the sts back onto original left-hand needle. K2tog, k1, k2tog. Loop is complete. Resume working remainder of Row 7.

Work one complete rep of 40 rows, then rep Rows 1 through 25 once more, making a loop each time you work Row 7.

Next row (WS): bind off 3 (5, 3, 5, 3, 5) sts, work in pat to end. You should now have 54 (54, 72, 72, 90, 90) sts.

Raglan shaping: beginning with Row 27, work shaping as follows:

Next row (RS): continue in pat as established to last 13 sts, p2tog, work 9 sts Braid Cable panel/chart (keeping continuity of braided cable pat as established), p2.

Next row (WS): p12, work in pat to end. Rep the last 2 rows 22 (22, 10, 10, 0, 0) times more, to 31 (31, 61, 61, 89, 89) sts.

Next row (RS): continue in pat as established to last 13 sts, p2tog, work 9 sts Braid Cable panel/chart, p2.

Next row (WS): p11, p2tog, work in pat to end. Rep the last 2 rows 2 (2, 17, 17, 31, 31) times more.

AT THE SAME TIME, continue working Main Pattern, until you have worked 2 complete 40-row repeats of pat, then work Rows 1 through 30 (30, 34, 34, 40, 40) once more.

Neck shaping (RS): Keeping continuity of pat and raglan shaping, shape neck edge as follows: p4, sl these 4 sts to safety pin, work in pat to end.

Next row (WS): work in pat to last 2 sts, p2tog.

Next row (RS): bind off 2 sts, work in pat to end. Rep last 2 rows once more. Hereafter, dec 1 st at neck edge on every row until you have 2 sts remaining. Break yarn and draw through last 2 sts to secure.

CARDIGAN LEFT FRONT

Cast on 51 (53, 69, 71, 87, 89) sts.

Work ribbing pat as follows:

RS rows: p2 (4, 2, 4, 2, 4), *k3, p3*, rep from * to last st, p1.

WS rows: p1, *p15, yo, p3, pass yo over last 3 sts*, rep from * to last 14 (16, 14, 16, 14, 16) sts, p to end.

Rep the last 2 rows until piece measures 8½" from bottom edge, ending with RS facing for next row.

Begin braided cable pat as follows:

Row 1 (RS): p2 (4, 2, 4, 2, 4), *C6F, [k3, p3] twice*, rep from * to last 13 sts, C6F, k3, p4.

Rows 2, 4, and 6 (WS): p1, *p15, yo, p3, pass yo over last 3 sts*, rep from * to last 14 (16, 14, 16, 14, 16) sts, p to end.

Rows 3 and 7 (RS): p2 (4, 2, 4, 2, 4), *k9, p3, k3, p3*, rep from * to last 13 sts, k9, p4.

Row 5 (RS): p2 (4, 2, 4, 2, 4), *k3, C6B, p3, k3, p3*, rep from * to last 13 sts, k3, C6B, p4.

Row 8 (WS): rep Row 2.

Rep Rows 1 through 6 once more.

Work prep rows for Main Pattern as follows, noting that 2 sts are increased on each RS row:

Prep Row 1 (RS): p2 (4, 2, 4, 2, 4), k3, *M1 purlwise, k3, M1 purlwise, k2, sl 1, k1, psso, p2, k3, p2, k2tog, k2*, rep from * 1 (1, 2, 2, 3, 3) time(s) more, [M1 purlwise, k3] twice, p4.

Prep Row 2 (WS): p4, *[p3, k1] twice, p5, yo, p3, pass yo over last 3 sts, p2*, rep from * 1 (1, 2, 2, 3, 3) time(s) more, [p3, k1] twice, p5 (7, 5, 7, 5, 7).

Prep Row 3 (RS): p2 (4, 2, 4, 2, 4), k3, *M1 purlwise, p1, k3, p1, M1 purlwise, k2, sl 1, k1, psso, p1, k3, p1, k2tog, k2*, rep from * 1 (1, 2, 2, 3, 3) time(s) more, M1 purlwise, p1, k3, p1, M1 purlwise, k3, p4.

Prep Row 4 (WS): p4, *[p3, k2] twice, p4, yo, p3, pass yo over last 3 sts, p1*, rep from * 1 (1, 2, 2, 3, 3) time(s) more, [p3, k2] twice, p5 (7, 5, 7, 5, 7).

Prep Row 5 (RS): p2 (4, 2, 4, 2, 4), k3, *M1 purlwise, p2, k3, p2, M1 purlwise, k2, sl 1, k1, psso, k3, k2tog, k2*, rep from * 1 (1, 2, 2, 3, 3) time(s) more, M1 purlwise, p2, k3, p2, M1 purlwise, k3, p4.

Prep Row 6 (WS): p7, *[k3, p3] twice, p6*, rep from * 1 (1, 2, 2, 3, 3) time(s) more, [k3, p3] twice, p2 (4, 2, 4, 2, 4).

You should now have 57 (59, 75, 77, 93, 95) sts.

Begin Main Pattern as follows:

Row 1 (RS): p2 (4, 2, 4, 2, 4), [work Row 1 of Main Pattern panel/chart, repeating directions between *...* 2 (2, 3, 3, 4, 4) times total, or working charted 18-st rep 2 (2, 3, 3, 4, 4) times total], p4.

Row 2 (WS): p4, [work Row 2 of Main Pattern panel/chart, repeating directions between *...* 2 (2, 3, 3, 4, 4) times total, or working charted 18-st rep 2 (2, 3, 3, 4, 4) times total], p2 (4, 2, 4, 2, 4).

Main Pattern is now in position. Continue working through remaining rows of panel, with purl sts at beginning and end of each row as noted in Rows 1 and 2, above. (There are no button loops on Left Front.)

Work one complete rep of 40 rows, then rep Rows 1 through 24 once more.

Next row (RS): bind off 3 (5, 3, 5, 3, 5) sts, work in pat to end. You should now have 54 (54, 72, 72, 90, 90) sts.

Raglan shaping: beginning with Row 26, work shaping as follows:

Next row (WS): work in pat to last 12 sts, p12.

Next row (RS): p2, work 9 sts Braid Cable panel/chart (keeping continuity of braided cable pat as established), p2tog, continue in pat to end. Rep the last 2 rows 22 (22, 10, 10, 0, 0) times more, to 31 (31, 61, 61, 89, 89) sts.

Next row (WS): cont in pat as established to last 13 sts, p2tog, p11.

Next row (RS): p2, work 9 sts Braid Cable panel/chart, p2tog, work in pat to end. Rep the last 2 rows 2 (2, 17, 17, 31, 31) times more.

AT THE SAME TIME, continue working Main Pattern, until you have worked 2 complete 40-row repeats of pat, then work Rows 1 through 29 (29, 33, 33, 39, 39) once more.

Neck shaping (WS): Keeping continuity of pat and raglan shaping, shape neck edge as follows: p4, sl these 4 sts to safety pin, work in pat to end.

Next row (RS): work in pat to last 2 sts, p2tog.

Next row (WS): bind off 2 sts, work in pat to end. Rep last 2 rows once more.

Hereafter, dec 1 st at neck edge on every row until you have 2 sts remaining. Break yarn and draw through last 2 sts to secure.

CARDIGAN BACK

Cast on 103 (107, 139, 143, 175, 179) sts.

Work ribbing pat as follows:

RS rows: p2 (4, 2, 4, 2, 4), k3, *p3, k3*, rep from * to last 2 (4, 2, 4, 2, 4) sts, p2 (4, 2, 4, 2, 4).

WS rows: p14 (16, 14, 16, 14, 16), *yo, p3, pass yo over last 3 sts, p15*, rep from * to last 17 (19, 17, 19, 17, 19) sts, yo, p3, pass yo over last 3 sts, p14 (16, 14, 16, 14, 16).

Rep the last 2 rows until piece measures 8½" from bottom edge, ending with RS facing for next row.

Begin braided cable patt as follows:

Row 1 (RS): p2 (4, 2, 4, 2, 4), *C6F, [k3, p3] twice*, rep from * to last 11 (13, 11, 13, 11, 13) sts, C6F, k3, p2 (4, 2, 4, 2, 4).

□	k on RS, p on WS	
−	p on RS, k on WS	
⋊	sl 1, k1, psso	
⋉	k2tog	
▽	M1 purlwise (see Special Abbreviations)	
⋈	yo, p3, pass yo over last 3 sts	
⟋	sl 3 to cable needle, hold to front, k3, k3 from cable needle	
⟍	sl 3 to cable needle, hold to back, k3, k3 from cable needle	

Main Pattern Chart

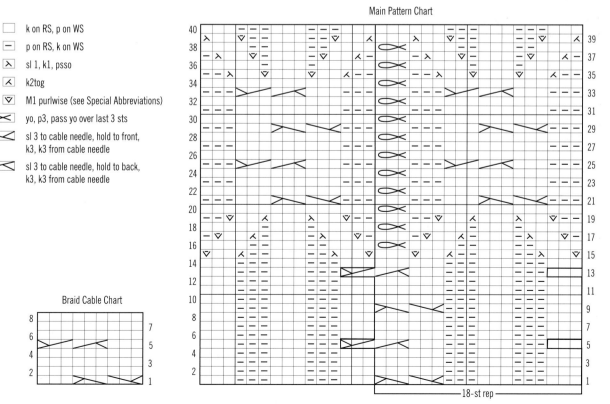

18-st rep

Braid Cable Chart

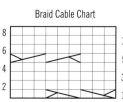

Rows 2, 4, and 6 (WS): p14 (16, 14, 16, 14, 16), *yo, p3, pass yo over last 3 sts, p15*, rep from * to last 17 (19, 17, 19, 17, 19) sts, yo, p3, pass yo over last 3 sts, p14 (16, 14, 16, 14, 16).

Rows 3 and 7 (RS): p2 (4, 2, 4, 2, 4), *k9, p3, k3, p3*, rep from * to last 11 (13, 11, 13, 11, 13) sts, k9, p2 (4, 2, 4, 2, 4).

Row 5 (RS): p2 (4, 2, 4, 2, 4), *k3, C6B, p3, k3, p3*, rep from * to last 11 (13, 11, 13, 11, 13) sts, k3, C6B, p2 (4, 2, 4, 2, 4).

Row 8 (WS): rep Row 2.

Rep Rows 1 through 6 once more.

Work prep rows for Main Pattern as follows, noting that 2 sts are increased on each RS row:

Prep Row 1 (RS): p2 (4, 2, 4, 2, 4), k3, *M1 purlwise, k3, M1 purlwise, k2, sl 1, k1, psso, p2, k3, p2, k2tog, k2*, rep from * 4 (4, 6, 6, 8, 8) times more, [M1 purlwise, k3] twice, p2 (4, 2, 4, 2, 4).

Prep Row 2 (WS): p2 (4, 2, 4, 2, 4), *[p3, k1] twice, p5, yo, p3, pass yo over last 3 sts, p2*, rep from * 4 (4, 6, 6, 8, 8) times more, [p3, k1] twice, p5 (7, 5, 7, 5, 7).

Prep Row 3 (RS): p2 (4, 2, 4, 2, 4), k3, *M1 purlwise, p1, k3, p1, M1 purl-wise, k2, sl 1, k1, psso, p1, k3, p1, k2tog, k2*, rep from * 4 (4, 6, 6, 8, 8) times more, M1 purlwise, p1, k3, p1, M1 purlwise, k3, p2 (4, 2, 4, 2, 4).

Prep Row 4 (WS): p2 (4, 2, 4, 2, 4), *[p3, k2] twice, p4, yo, p3, pass yo over last 3 sts, p1*, rep from * 4 (4, 6, 6, 8, 8) times more, [p3, k2] twice, p5 (7, 5, 7, 5, 7).

Prep Row 5 (RS): p2 (4, 2, 4, 2, 4), k3, *M1 purlwise, p2, k3, p2, M1 purlwise, k2, sl 1, k1, psso, k3, k2tog, k2*, rep from * 4 (4, 6, 6, 8, 8) times more, M1 purlwise, p2, k3, p2, M1 purlwise, k3, p2 (4, 2, 4, 2, 4).

Prep Row 6 (WS): p2 (4, 2, 4, 2, 4), *[p3, k3] twice, p6*, rep from * 4 (4, 6, 6, 8, 8) times more, [p3, k3] twice, p5 (7, 5, 7, 5, 7).

You should now have 109 (113, 145, 149, 181, 185) sts.

Begin Main Pattern as follows:

Row 1 (RS): p2 (4, 2, 4, 2, 4), [work Row 1 of Main Pattern panel/chart, repeating directions between *...* 5 (5, 7, 7, 9, 9) times total, or working charted 18-st rep 5 (5, 7, 7, 9, 9) times total], p2 (4, 2, 4, 2, 4).

Row 2 (WS): p2 (4, 2, 4, 2, 4), [work Row 2 of Main Pattern panel/chart, repeating directions between *...* 5 (5, 7, 7, 9, 9) times total or working charted 18-st rep 5 (5, 7, 7, 9, 9) times total], p2 (4, 2, 4, 2, 4).

Main Pattern is now in position. Continue working through remaining rows of panel/chart, with purl sts at beginning and end of each row as noted in Rows 1 and 2, above.

Work one complete rep of 40 rows, then rep Rows 1 through 24 once more.

Bind off 3 (5, 3, 5, 3, 5) sts at beg of next 2 rows, work in pat to end. You should now have 103 (103, 139, 139, 175, 175) sts.

Raglan shaping: beginning with Row 27, work shaping as follows:

Next row (RS): p2, work 9 sts Braid Cable panel/chart (keeping continuity of braided cable pat as established), p2tog, continue in Main Pattern as established to last 13 sts, p2tog, work 9 sts Braid Cable panel/chart, p2.

Next row (WS): p12, work in pat to last 12 sts, p12. Rep the last 2 rows 22 (22, 10, 10, 0, 0) times more, to 57 (57, 117, 117, 173, 173) sts.

Next row (RS): p2, work 9 sts Braid Cable panel/chart, p2tog, cont in pat as established to last 13 sts, p2tog, work 9 sts Braid Cable panel/chart, p2.

Next row (WS): p11, p2tog, work in pat to last 13 sts, p2tog, p11. Rep the last 2 rows, to 45 sts.

Work even, if necessary, until length of raglan seam matches length of Front raglan seam to tip, ending with RS facing for next row. Leave remaining 45 sts on spare needle or holder.

CARDIGAN SLEEVES

Cast on 49 (53, 67, 71, 85, 89) sts and work ribbing pat as given for Back until piece measures 3" from bottom edge, ending with RS facing for next row.

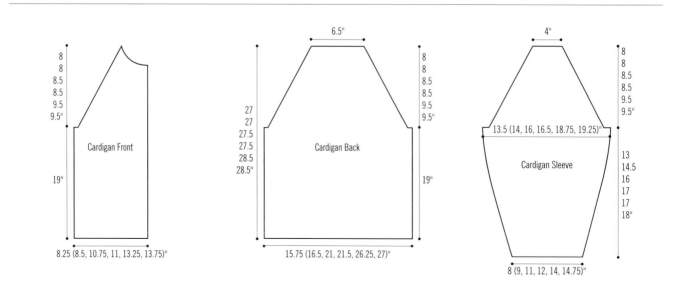

Cardigan Front

8
8
8.5
8.5
9.5
9.5"

19"

8.25 (8.5, 10.75, 11, 13.25, 13.75)"

6.5"

27
27
27.5
27.5
28.5
28.5"

Cardigan Back

8
8
8.5
8.5
9.5
9.5"

19"

15.75 (16.5, 21, 21.5, 26.25, 27)"

4"

8
8
8.5
8.5
9.5
9.5"

13.5 (14, 16, 16.5, 18.75, 19.25)"

Cardigan Sleeve

13
14.5
16
17
17
18"

8 (9, 11, 12, 14, 14.75)"

Work 14 rows braided cable pat as given for Back on page 57, then work 6 prep rows as given for Back, working directions between *...* 3 times. You should now have 55 (59, 73, 77, 91, 95) sts.

Begin Main Pattern as follows:

Row 1 (RS): p2 (4, 2, 4, 2, 4), [work Row 1 of Main Pattern panel/chart, repeating directions between *...* 2 (2, 3, 3, 4, 4) times total, or working 18-st rep 2 (2, 3, 3, 4, 4) times total], p2 (4, 2, 4, 2, 4).

Row 2 (WS): p2 (4, 2, 4, 2, 4), [work Row 2 of Main Pattern panel/chart, repeating directions between *...* 2 (2, 3, 3, 4, 4) times total, or working 18-st rep 2 (2, 3, 3, 4, 4) times total], p2 (4, 2, 4, 2, 4).

Main Pattern is now in position. Continue working through remaining rows of panel/chart, with purl sts at beginning and end of each row as noted in Rows 1 and 2, above. Rep 40-row pat as needed until piece measures 13 (14½, 16, 17, 17, 18)" from bottom edge.

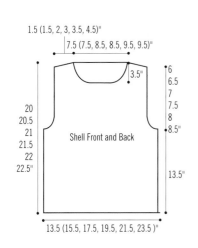

1.5 (1.5, 2, 3, 3.5, 4.5)"

7.5 (7.5, 8.5, 8.5, 9.5, 9.5)"

3.5"

6
6.5
7
7.5
8
8.5"

20
20.5
21
21.5
22
22.5"

Shell Front and Back

13.5"

13.5 (15.5, 17.5, 19.5, 21.5, 23.5)"

AT THE SAME TIME, inc 1 st at each end of every 2nd row 7 (5, 3, 7, 7, 5) times, then every 4th row, placing your incs 2 (4, 2, 4, 2, 4) sts away from edges and making your incs in pat. Make a total of 18 incs per side, thus adding two full pattern repeats, to 91 (95, 109, 113, 127, 131) sts.

Bind off 3 (5, 3, 5, 3, 5) sts at beginning of next 2 rows, work in pat to end. You should now have 85 (85, 103, 103, 121, 121) sts.

Raglan shaping (RS): p2, work 9 sts Braid Cable panel/chart, p2tog, continue in pat as established to last 13 sts, p2tog, work 9 sts Braid Cable panel/chart, p2.

Next row (WS): p12, work in pat to last 12 sts, p12. Rep the last 2 rows 28 (28, 26, 26, 25, 25) times more, to 27 (27, 49, 49, 69, 69) sts.

Next row (RS): p2, work 9 sts Braid Cable panel/chart (keeping continuity of braided cable pat as established), p2tog, continue in pat as established to last 13 sts, p2tog, work 9 sts Braid Cable panel/chart, p2.

Next row (WS): p11, p2tog, work in pat to last 13 sts, p2tog, p11. Rep the last 2 rows, to 25 sts. Work even, if necessary, until length of raglan seam matches length of Front raglan seam, ending with RS facing for next row. Sl sts to holder.

SHELL

FRONT

Cast on 81 (93, 105, 117, 129, 141) sts.

Work ribbing pat as follows:

RS rows: k3, *p3, k3*, rep from * to end.

WS rows: p12 (18, 24, 30, 36, 42), *yo, p3, pass yo over last 3 sts, p15*, rep from * twice more, .yo, p3, pass yo over last 3 sts, p12 (18, 24, 30, 36, 42).

Rep the last 2 rows until piece measures 13½" from bottom edge, ending with RS facing for next row.

Armhole shaping: bind off 3 sts at beginning of the next 2 rows.

Next row (RS): p3, sl 1, k1, psso, work pat to last 5 sts, k2tog, p3.

Next row (WS): work pat to end. Rep the last 2 rows 5 (11, 11, 11, 11, 11) more times, to 63 (63, 75, 87, 99, 111) sts.

Work even in pat until length measures 16½ (17, 17½, 18, 18½, 19)" from bottom edge, ending with RS facing for next row. Read through remaining Front directions before proceeding.

Left side neck shaping: work 24 (24, 30, 36, 42, 48) sts in pat. Turn, leaving remaining sts on spare needle or holder.

Next row (WS): bind off 5 (5, 7, 7, 7, 7) sts, work pat to end.

Next row (RS): work pat to last 2 sts, dec 1 (either k2tog or p2tog to keep continuity of pat).

Next row (WS): bind off 3 sts, work pat to end. Rep the last 2 rows 1 (1, 1, 1, 2, 2) more time(s). Hereafter, dec 1 st at end of each RS row and bind off 1 st at beginning of each WS row until you have 9 (9, 12, 18, 21, 27) sts remaining for shoulder.

Work even until length measures 6 (6½, 7, 7½, 8, 8½)" from beginning of arm-hole shaping, ending with RS facing for next row.

Left shoulder shaping (RS): bind off 3 (3, 4, 6, 7, 9) sts, work pat to end.

Next row (WS): work pat. Rep the last 2 rows once more.

Next row (RS): bind off remaining 3 (3, 4, 6, 7, 9) sts.

Right side neck shaping: with RS facing, leave first 15 sts on stitch holder. Join yarn to next st and bind off 5 (5, 7, 7, 7, 7) sts, work pat to end.

Next row (WS): work pat to last 2 sts, dec 1 (either k2tog or p2tog to keep continuity of pat).

Next row (RS): bind off 3 sts, work pat to end. Rep the last 2 rows 1 (1, 1, 1, 2, 2) more time(s). Hereafter, dec 1 st at end of each WS row and bind off 1 st at beginning of each RS row until you have 9 (9, 12, 18, 21, 27) sts remaining for shoulder.

Work even until length measures 6 (6½, 7, 7½, 8, 8½)" from beginning of arm-hole shaping, ending with WS facing for next row.

Right shoulder shaping (WS): bind off 3 (3, 4, 6, 7, 9) sts, work pat to end.

Next row (RS): work pat.

Rep the last 2 rows once more.

Next row (WS): bind off remaining 3 (3, 4, 6, 7, 9) sts.

SHELL BACK

Work as given for Front up to and including armhole shaping.

Work even in pat until length measures 6 (6½, 7, 7½, 8, 8½)" from beginning of armhole shaping, ending with RS facing for next row.

Shoulder shaping: working in pat, bind off 3 (3, 4, 6, 7, 9) sts at beginning of next 6 rows. Leave remaining 45 (45, 51, 51, 57, 57) sts for Back neck on a spare needle or holder.

CARDIGAN

Block pieces as directed in gauge swatch, to measurements shown. Sew sleeve seams and side seams. Sew raglan seams.

Neckband: with RS facing, tie on yarn and knit across 4 sts from Right Front safety pin; pick up and knit 18 sts along Right Front neck edge; work 25 sts from first Sleeve holder as follows: k5, [k2tog, k3] 4 times; work 45 sts from Back st holder as follows: k1, [k2tog, k2] 11 times; work 25 sts from second Sleeve holder as follows: [k3, k2tog] 4 times, k5; pick up and knit 18 sts along Left Front neck edge; knit across 4 sts from Left Front safety pin, for 120 sts total. Work 6 rows garter st (k all sts on all rows). Bind off.

Sew 3 buttons to correspond to button loops. To prevent buttons from pulling the fabric, place small sew-through button on WS of garment behind large button, and sew through both buttons to join.

SHELL

Block pieces as directed in gauge swatch, to measurements shown. Sew right shoulder seam.

Collar: with RS facing, pick up and knit 24 (24, 27, 27, 30, 30) sts down left Front neck edge, work pat across 15 sts on Front neck stitch holder, pick up and knit 24 (24, 27, 27, 30, 30) sts up right Front neck edge, and work pat across 45 (45, 51, 51, 57, 57) sts from Back neck stitch holder. You should have 108 (108, 120, 120, 132, 132) sts.

Next row (WS): p3 (3, 0, 0, 3, 3), *k3, p3*, rep from * to last 3 (3, 0, 0, 3, 3) sts, k3 (3, 0, 0, 3, 3).

Next row (RS): p3 (3, 0, 0, 3, 3), *k3, p3*, rep from * to last 3 (3, 0, 0, 3, 3) sts, k3 (3, 0, 0, 3, 3). Rep the last 2 rows until collar measures 3½" from beginning, ending with RS facing for next row. Bind off in pat.

Sew collar seam and left shoulder seam. Sew side seams. ❧

pronto

This design is as close to instant gratification as it gets. Worked on 15 mm needles in basic garter stitch and stocking stitch, it's perfect for a novice knitter. The simple, straight shapes knit up quickly in this amazing yarn – a lightweight wool that's braided for a subtle texture. The standaway collar and updated silhouette make it a nice choice for both teens and adults.

SKILL LEVEL: VERY EASY

MEASUREMENTS

SIZES (in inches)	TEENS			WOMEN			
	12	14	16	SM	MD	LG	XL
Finished Bust	32	35	38	40	43	46	49
Finshed Length	16	17	18	19	20	21	22

MATERIALS

Yarn: Naturally Tibet 99% Wool 1% Elastane #04 (51 yds or 47 m/50 gr ball). *See also page 126 for yarn information.*

NO. OF BALLS	TEENS			WOMEN			
	12	14	16	SM	MD	LG	XL
#04	9	10	11	12	14	15	16

Needles: 1 pr. 15 mm needles OR SIZE TO OBTAIN GAUGE

Spare needle or stitch holder (you can use loops of contrasting yarn)

GAUGE

9 sts = 4" in garter st and st st

To work Gauge Swatch: cast on 12 sts and work garter st (k all sts on all rows) until piece measures 2" from bottom edge, then change to st st (k all sts on RS and p all sts on WS) and work until piece measures 6" from bottom edge. Bind off. Block swatch by laying flat and applying lots of steam with steam iron held just above the swatch. Let cool and dry. If you have too many sts to the inch, switch to a larger needle; too few means you should use a smaller needle. You may need to use different needle sizes for the garter st and st st to obtain gauge.

Your garment will not fit properly if the tension gauge is incorrect! Take the time to check by making gauge swatch.

Directions are given for Teens' size 12. Teens' sizes 14, 16, and Women's sizes Small, Medium, Large, and Extra-Large are given in parentheses. Where there is only one number, it applies to all sizes.

FRONT

Cast on 36 (40, 42, 46, 48, 52, 56) sts.

Work st st until piece measures 10 (10½, 11, 11½, 12, 12½, 13)" from bottom edge, ending with RS facing for next row.

Armhole shaping: cont in st st and bind off 1 st at beginning of every row 4 (4, 4, 5, 5, 5, 6) times on each side. You should now have 28 (32, 34, 36, 38, 42, 44) sts remaining.

Continue in st st until piece measures 3 (3½, 4, 4½, 5, 5½, 6)" from beginning of armhole shaping, ending with RS facing for next row.

Left neck shaping: k11 (12, 13, 13, 14, 16, 16). Turn, leaving remaining sts on spare needle or stitch holder.

Next row (WS): bind off 3 sts, p to end.

Next row (RS): k to last 2 sts, k2tog. Hereafter, bind off 1 st at beginning of every WS row until you have 5 (6, 7, 7, 8, 9, 9) sts remaining for shoulder. Work even (no decs) until piece measures 6 (6½, 7, 7½, 8, 8½, 9)" from beginning of armhole shaping, ending with RS facing for next row. Bind off.

Right neck shaping: with RS facing, join yarn to first st and bind off 6 (8, 8, 10, 10, 10, 12) sts, then k to end.

Next row (WS): p to last 2 sts, p2tog.

Next row (RS): bind off 3 sts, k to end. Hereafter, bind off 1 st at beginning of every RS row until you have 5 (6, 7, 7, 8, 9, 9) sts remaining for shoulder. Work even (no decs) until piece measures 6 (6½, 7, 7½, 8, 8½, 9)" from beginning of armhole shaping, ending with RS facing for next row. Bind off.

BACK

Work as for Front, including armhole shaping, but omitting neck shaping as follows: work even after completing armhole shaping, until piece measures 6 (6½, 7, 7½, 8, 8½, 9)" from beginning of armhole shaping, ending with RS facing for next row. Bind off 5 (6, 7, 7, 8, 9, 9) sts at the beginning of each of the next 2 rows. Leave remaining 18 (20, 20, 22, 22, 24, 26) sts for back neck on a stitch holder.

SLEEVES

Cast on 20 (24, 26, 28, 28, 30, 30) sts. Work garter st (k all sts on all rows) until piece measures 2" from bottom edge, ending with RS facing for next row.

Proceed in st st; AT THE SAME TIME, shape sleeve by inc 1 at each side on 11th (11th, 11th, 11th, 9th, 9th, 7th) row and every 12th (12th, 12th, 12th, 10th, 10th, 8th) row thereafter, until you have 26 (30, 32, 34, 36, 38, 40) sts.

Work even (no incs) in st st until piece measures 15½ (16, 16½, 16½, 17, 17, 17)" from bottom edge, ending with RS facing for next row.

Cap shaping: continue in st st and bind off 1 st at beginning of every row for 8 (8, 8, 10, 10, 10, 12) rows, thus ending with 18 (22, 24, 24, 26, 28, 28) sts and RS facing for next row. Bind off all remaining sts.

FINISHING

Block pieces as directed in gauge swatch, to measurements shown. Sew right shoulder seam.

Collar: with RS facing, pick up and knit 13 (14, 14, 15, 15, 16, 17) sts along left Front neck edge, pick up and knit 13 (14, 14, 15, 15, 16, 17) sts along right Front neck edge, and knit across 18 (20, 20, 22, 22, 24, 26) sts from Back neck stitch holder. You should have a total of 44 (48, 48, 52, 52, 56, 60) sts. Work garter st until collar measures 4" from beginning, ending with RS facing for next row. Bind off.

Sew left shoulder seam and collar seam. Sew sleeve seams and side seams. Set in sleeves, matching armhole shaping to cap shaping. ❧

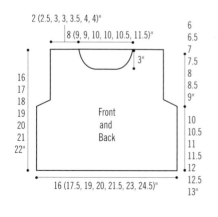
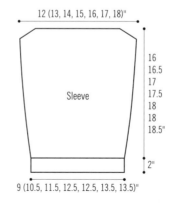

2 (2.5, 3, 3, 3.5, 4, 4)"
8 (9, 9, 10, 10, 10.5, 11.5)"
6
6.5
7
3"
7.5
8
8.5
9"
16
17
18
19
20
21
22"
Front and Back
10
10.5
11
11.5
12
12.5
13"
16 (17.5, 19, 20, 21.5, 23, 24.5)"

12 (13, 14, 15, 16, 17, 18)"
Sleeve
16
16.5
17
17.5
18
18
18.5"
2"
9 (10.5, 11.5, 12.5, 12.5, 13.5, 13.5)"

QUICK TIP: *When you're making increases at the side seams of a piece, as required on most sleeves, work your increases one stitch away from the edge for a smoother seam.*

whistler

Nordic ski sweaters are classic examples of the knitter's art, incorporating almost-abstract snowflake motifs and geometric patterns that go back for generations. To reinterpret this tradition and give it a fresh look, I designed this pullover with snowflake bands that point down from the neck and run along the saddle shoulder, intersecting with borders that repeat on the sweater's edges.

SKILL LEVEL: INTERMEDIATE

MEASUREMENTS

SIZES (in inches)	TEENS			ADULTS			
	12	14	16	SM	MD	LG	XL
Finished Chest	32	36	40	44	48	52	56
Finished Length	23	24	25	26	26½	27	27½
Finished Cap Circumference	20	20	20	22	22	22	22

MATERIALS

Yarn: Galway Highland 100% Pure Virgin Wool (230 yds or 212 m/100 gr ball). *See also page 126 for yarn information.*

NO. OF BALLS	TEENS			ADULTS			
	12	14	16	SM	MD	LG	XL
MC: Teal #726	3	3	4	4	5	5	6
A: Greymix #702	2	2	2	3	3	4	4
B: Navy #705	2	2	3	3	3	3	4
C: Purple #732	1	1	1	1	1	1	1
D: Burgundy #727	1	1	1	1	1	1	1

Note: to work the two-color version shown on page 68, replace colors MC, B, C, and D with 4 (4, 5, 6, 6, 7, 8) balls of desired background color.

Needles: 1 pr. each U.S. sizes 6 and 7 (4 mm and 4.5 mm) needles OR SIZE TO OBTAIN GAUGE

Spare needles or stitch holders

GAUGE

20 sts and 23 rows= 4" in charted pattern using larger needles

To work Gauge Swatch: with MC and larger needles, cast on 25 sts and work Chart 2, working 5 st-rep 5 times across row and repeating 12 rows of chart until piece measures 4" long. Knit RS rows and purl WS rows, reading RS rows of chart from right to left and WS rows from left to right, and carry out-of-work color across WS. Bind off. Block swatch by laying flat and applying lots of steam with steam iron held just above the swatch. Let cool and dry. If you have too many sts and rows to the inch, switch to a larger needle; too few means you should use a smaller needle.

Your garment will not fit properly if the tension gauge is incorrect! Take the time to check by making gauge swatch.

Directions are given for Teens' size 12. Teens' sizes 14, 16, and Adults' sizes Small, Medium, Large, and Extra-Large are given in parentheses. Where there is only one number, it applies to all sizes.

FRONT

With smaller needles and MC, cast on 81 (91, 101, 111, 121, 131, 141) sts.

Begin Chart I, reading RS rows from right to left and WS rows from left to right and noting that some sts are knitted on WS as indicated on chart (though the out-of-work color is always carried across the WS of work):

Row 1 (RS): work 10-st rep 8 (9, 10, 11, 12, 13, 14) times across row, end with st #1.

Row 2 (WS): work st #1, then work 10-st rep 8 (9, 10, 11, 12, 13, 14) times across row.

Charted pat is now in position; work to end of Chart I.

Change to larger needles and work remainder of Front in st st as follows:

Begin Chart II:

Row 1 (RS): work 5-st rep 16 (18, 20, 22, 24, 26, 28) times across row, end with st #1.

Row 2 (WS): work st #1, then work 5-st rep 16 (18, 20, 22, 24, 26, 28) times across row.

Charted pat is now in position; work to end of Chart II, then rep the 12 rows of Chart II until piece measures as close as possible to 11 (11½, 12½, 13, 13, 13, 13)" from bottom edge, while ending with Row 2 of chart.

Begin Yoke, starting at Row 1 of Chart III and placing reps as follows:

Row 1 (RS): work st #1 (6, 1, 6, 1, 6, 1) through st #10, work 10-st Left panel 2 (3, 3, 4, 4, 5, 5) times, work 21-st Center panel, work 10-st Right panel 2 (3, 3, 4, 4, 5, 5) times, then work st #32 through st #41 (36, 41, 36, 41, 36, 41).

Row 2 (WS): work st #41 (36, 41, 36, 41, 36, 41) through st #32, work 10-st Right panel 2 (3, 3, 4, 4, 5, 5) times, work 21-st Center panel, work 10-st Left panel 2 (3, 3, 4, 4, 5, 5) times, work st #10 through st #1 (6, 1, 6, 1, 6, 1).

Charted pat is now in position; continue working Chart III as established until Row 22 of chart is complete.

Armhole Shaping:

Next row (RS): with A, bind off 10 sts, sl st remaining from bind offs back to left-hand needle and work Row 23 of Chart III as follows: work st #1 (6, 1, 6, 1, 6, 1) through st #10, work 10-st Left panel 1 (2, 2, 3, 3, 4, 4) times, work 21-st Center panel, work 10-st Right panel 1 (2, 2, 3, 3, 4, 4) times, work st #32 through st #41 (36, 41, 36, 41, 36, 41); with A, k to end.

Next row (WS): with A, bind off 10 sts, sl st remaining from bind offs back to left-hand needle and work Row 24 of Chart III as follows: work st #41 (36, 41, 36, 41, 36, 41) through st #32, work 10-st Right panel 1 (2, 2, 3, 3, 4, 4) times, work 21-st Center panel, work

10-st Left panel 1 (2, 2, 3, 3, 4, 4) times, work st #10 through st #1 (6, 1, 6, 1, 6, 1). You should now have 61 (71, 81, 91, 101, 111, 121) sts remaining.

Work even to end of Chart III with placement as established, then rep Rows 23 through 52 until piece measures 5 (5½, 5½, 6, 6½, 7, 7½)" from armhole shaping, ending with RS facing for next row.

Left neck shaping: work 23 (28, 31, 36, 41, 45, 50) sts in pat. Turn, leaving remaining sts on spare needle or stitch holder. Keeping continuity of charted pat, shape neck edge as follows:

Next row (WS): bind off 2 sts, work pat to end.

Next row (RS): work pat to last 2 sts, k2tog.

Next row (WS): bind off 1 st, work pat to end.

Next row (RS): work pat to end. Rep last 2 rows 0 (0, 0, 0, 0, 1, 1) more time until you have 19 (24, 27, 32, 37, 40, 45) sts remaining for left shoulder. Work even, if necessary, until piece measures 6 (6½, 6½, 7, 7½, 8, 8½)" from armhole bind offs, ending with RS facing for next row. With A, bind off.

Right neck shaping; with larger needles and RS facing, join yarn to first st and bind off 15 (15, 19, 19, 19, 21, 21) sts, then work in pat to end of row. Keeping continuity of charted pat, shape neck edge as follows:

Next row (WS): work pat to last 2 sts, p2tog.

Next row (RS): bind off 2 sts, work pat to end.

Next row (WS): work pat to end.

Next row (RS): bind off 1 st, work pat to end. Rep last 2 rows 0 (0, 0, 0, 0, 1, 1) more time until you have 19 (24, 27, 32, 37, 40, 45) sts remaining for right shoulder. Work even, if necessary, until piece measures 6 (6½, 6½, 7, 7½, 8, 8½)" from armhole bind offs, ending with RS facing for next row. With A, bind off.

BACK

Work exactly as given for Front to "Left neck shaping."

Work even in pat until length of piece matches length of Front to shoulder, ending with RS facing for next row. With A, bind off.

SLEEVES

With smaller needles and MC, cast on 41 (41, 41, 51, 51, 61, 61) sts.

Begin Chart I:

Row 1 (RS): work 10-st rep 4 (4, 4, 5, 5, 6, 6) times across row, end with st #1.

Row 2 (WS): work st #1, then work 10-st rep 4 (4, 4, 5, 5, 6, 6) times across row.

Charted pat is now in position; work to end of Chart I.

Change to larger needles.

Begin Chart II, working in st st:

Row 1 (RS): work 5-st rep 8 (8, 8, 10, 10, 12, 12) times across row, end with st #1.

Row 2 (WS): work st #1, then work 5-st rep 8 (8, 8, 10, 10, 12, 12) times across row.

Charted pat is now in position; work to end of chart, rep the 12 rows of chart 3 more times; AT THE SAME TIME, inc 1 st at each side on 3rd row, then every following 4th row until you have 65 (65, 65, 75, 75, 85, 85) sts. Due to an error in the sweater shown in photo, your background color will vary at this point from color shown in photo.

Begin Chart III, still working in st st and placing pat as follows:

Chart III

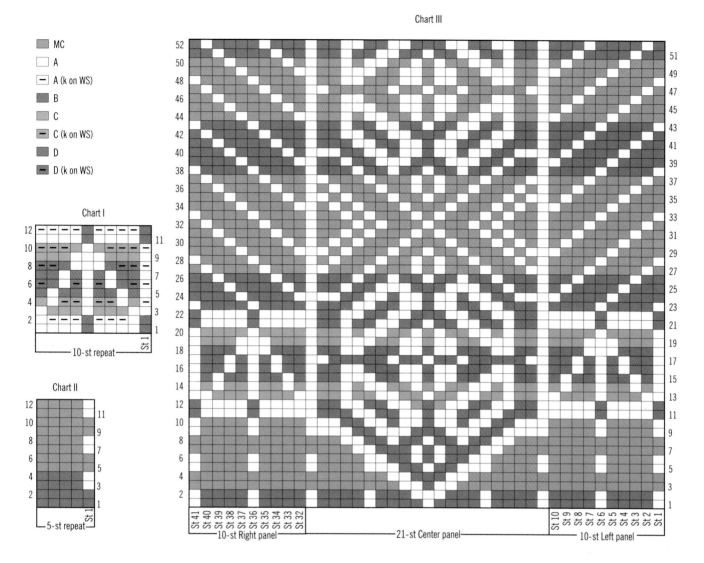

Legend:
- MC
- A
- A (k on WS)
- B
- C
- C (k on WS)
- D
- D (k on WS)

Chart I

10-st repeat

Chart II

5-st repeat

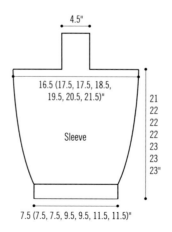

4 (5, 5.5, 6.5, 7.5, 8, 9)"

4.5 (4.5, 5.5, 5.5, 5.5, 6, 6)"

1"

6
6.5
6.5
7
7.5
8
8.5"

21
22
23
24
24.5
25
25.5"

Front and Back

15
15.5
16.5
17
17
17
17"

16 (18, 20, 22, 24, 26, 28)"
Note: Finished body length
incl. saddle shoulder = 23 (24, 25, 26, 26.5, 27, 27.5)"

4.5"

16.5 (17.5, 17.5, 18.5, 19.5, 20.5, 21.5)"

Sleeve

21
22
22
22
23
23
23"

7.5 (7.5, 7.5, 9.5, 9.5, 11.5, 11.5)"

QUICK TIP: *Learning to work Fair Isle patterns with two hands, carrying one color in each hand, takes a little patience, but eventually you'll be gratified by how much faster you can knit.*

Row 1 (RS): work st #9 (9, 9, 4, 4, 9, 9) through st #10, work 10-st left panel 2 (2, 2, 2, 2, 3, 3) times, work 21-st Center panel, work 10-st Right panel 2 (2, 2, 2, 2, 3, 3) times, then work st #32 through st #33 (33, 33, 38, 38, 33, 33).

Row 2 (WS): work st #33 (33, 33, 38, 38, 33, 33) through st #32, work 10-st Right panel 2 (2, 2, 2, 2, 3, 3) times, work 21-st Center panel, work 10-st Left panel 2 (2, 2, 2, 2, 3, 3) times, work st #10 through st #9 (9, 9, 4, 4, 9, 9).

Charted pat is now in position; work to end of chart, then rep Rows 23 through 52, resuming incs at each side every 4th row until you have 83 (87, 87, 93, 97, 103, 107) sts.

Work even in pat until piece measures 21 (22, 22, 22, 23, 23, 23)" from bottom edge, ending with RS facing for next row.

Saddle shoulder extension: keeping continuity of pat, bind off 30 (32, 32, 35, 37, 40, 42) sts at beginning of the next 2 rows. You should now have 23 sts remaining.

Next row (RS): k1 with A, work 21-st Center panel to last st, k1 with A. Working first and last sts in A st st, continue working 21-st Center panel until length of extension matches width of Front shoulder, ending with RS facing for next row. With A, bind off.

FINISHING

Sew saddle shoulder extensions to Front and Back shoulders, leaving right back shoulder seam open for collar.

Collar: With larger needles, RS of garment facing, and A, pick up and knit 25 (25, 29, 29, 29, 33, 33) sts across Back neck edge, pick up and knit 19 sts across top of left saddle shoulder, pick up and knit 28 (28, 34, 34, 34, 40, 40) sts along Front neck edge, and pick up and knit 19 sts along top of right saddle shoulder, to 91 (91, 101, 101, 101, 111, 111) sts. Beginning with Row 2, work Chart I until Row 5 is complete, placing pat as follows: work 10-st rep 9 (9, 10, 10, 10, 11, 11) times, end with st #1. At beginning of Row 6, change to smaller needles and work until chart is complete. With A, bind off all sts.

Sew collar seam and left back saddle shoulder seam. Sew tops of sleeves to armholes. Sew upper sleeve seams to armhole bound-off sts. Sew side seams and sleeve seams.

CAP

With larger needles and MC, cast on 101 (111) sts.

Begin Chart I:

Row 1 (RS): work 10-st rep 10 (11) times across row, end with st #1.

Row 2 (WS): work st #1, then work 10 = st rep 10 (11) times across row.

Charted pat is now in position; work to end of Chart I.

Begin Chart II, working in st st:

Row 1 (RS): work 5-st rep 20 (22) times across row, end with st #1.

Row 2 (WS): work st #1, then work 5-st rep 20 (22) times across row.

Charted pat is now in position; work to end of chart, then work Rows 1 through 4 once more.

Begin shaping, working st st in MC:

Row 1 (RS): *k18 (20), k2tog*, rep from * 4 more times, k1.

Row 2 (WS): purl.

Row 3 (RS): *k17 (19), k2tog*, rep from * 4 more times, k1.

Row 4 (WS): purl.

Continue in this manner, working one less st between each dec on every following RS row, until you have worked 14 rows total in MC. You should now have 66 (76) sts remaining.

Next row (RS): k2tog across row.

Next row (WS): p2tog across row. Break yarn, leaving a long tail, and draw through remaining sts and fasten securely. Sew cap seam. ❧

softy

Both versions of this easy design are worked in plush, soft yarns on big needles – the women's longer coat with optional self-belt and pockets is shown in a luxurious alpaca blend, and the teens' cropped version uses a fluffy mohair yarn, gorgeously variegated in stained-glass colors.

SKILL LEVEL: VERY EASY

MEASUREMENTS

SIZES (in inches)	TEENS			WOMEN			
	12	14	16	SM	MD	LG	XL
Finished Bust	32	36	40	41.5	47	50	53
Finished Length	14½	15½	16½	27	27½	28	28½

MATERIALS

Yarn: Teens' version – King Cole Luxury Mohair 78% Mohair, 13% Wool, 9% Nylon #259 (109 yds or 101 m/50 gr ball).
Yarn: Women's version – Schachenmayr Piano 42% Alpaca, 40% Nylon, 18% Wool #03 (87 yds or 80 m/50 gr ball).
See also page 126 for yarn information.

NO. OF BALLS	TEENS			WOMEN			
	12	14	16	SM	MD	LG	XL
#259 or #03	5	6	7	13	14	16	17

Needles: 1 pr. U.S. size 9 (5.5 mm) needles OR SIZE TO OBTAIN GAUGE

1 pr. U.S. size 8 (5 mm) needles for pockets on women's version

Spare needles or stitch holders

Stitch markers (or safety pin)

SPECIAL ABBREVIATIONS

triple dec = insert needle from left to right into next 2 sts at once and sl to right-hand needle, k1, pass 2 slipped sts over last-knitted st.

GAUGE

15 sts and 22 rows = 4" in st st using larger needles and either yarn

To work Gauge Swatch (for either version): with larger needles, cast on 25 sts and work ribbing for 8 rows as follows:

RS rows: k1, *p1, k1*, rep from * to end.

WS rows: purl.

Change to st st (k all sts on RS and p all sts on WS) and work until piece measures 5" from bottom edge. Bind off. Do not block. If you have too many sts and rows to the inch, switch to a larger needle; too few means you should use a smaller needle.

Your garment will not fit properly if the tension gauge is incorrect! Take the time to check by making gauge swatch.

Directions are given for Teens' size 12. Teens' sizes 14, 16, and Women's sizes Small, Medium, Large, and Extra-Large are given in parentheses. Where there is only one number, it applies to all sizes.

BACK

With larger needles, cast on 61 (67, 75, 93, 99, 103, 107) sts.

Work 12 rows of ribbing as given for Gauge Swatch.

WOMEN'S VERSION – SM (MD, LG, XL)

Change to st st; AT THE SAME TIME, working decs on 13th row as follows: k1, sl 1, k1, psso, k to last 3 sts, k2tog, k1.

Continue working st st with decs every 12th row until you have 81 (87, 91, 95) sts remaining (12 sts decreased).

Work even (no decs) until piece measures 17½" from bottom edge, ending with RS facing for next row.

TEENS' VERSION – 12 (14, 16)

Change to st st and work until piece measures 6½ (7, 7½)" from bottom edge, ending with RS facing for next row.

BOTH VERSIONS

Armhole shaping: continuing in st st, bind off sts at beginning of each row in the following sequence: bind off 3 sts once per side, then bind off 2 sts once per side, then bind off 1 st 3 times per side. You should have bound off a total of 8 sts each at both edges of the piece, to 45 (51, 59, 65, 71, 75, 79) sts remaining.

Continue in st st until piece measures 13½ (14½, 15½, 26, 26½, 27, 27½)" from bottom edge, ending with RS facing for next row.

Shoulder shaping: continuing in st st, bind off 4 (5, 7, 7, 8, 9, 9) sts at beginning of next 2 rows, then bind off 3 (4, 5, 6, 7, 7, 8) sts at beginning of next 4 rows. Leave remaining 25 (25, 25, 27, 27, 29, 29) sts for neck on a spare needle or holder.

POCKET

Make 2, for Women's Version only.

With smaller needles, cast on 21 sts and work st st until piece measures 7" from bottom edge, ending with RS facing for next row.

Next row (RS): k7, *k2tog, k5*, rep from * once more, to 19 sts. Leave sts on needle, to be picked up when working fronts.

LEFT FRONT

With larger needles, cast on 29 (33, 37, 47, 51, 55, 59) sts.

Work 12 rows of ribbing as given for Gauge Swatch.

WOMEN'S VERSION – SM (MD, LG, XL)

Begin working pat as follows:

RS rows: k to last 6 sts, *p1, k1*, rep from * twice more.

WS rows: purl.

Rep the last 2 rows; AT THE SAME TIME, shaping side seam (right-hand edge on RS) on 13th row, and every 12th row thereafter as follows: k1, sl 1, k1, psso, k to last 6 sts, *p1, k1*, rep from * twice more.

Continue in pat as established until you have 44 (48, 52, 56) sts.

Next row (WS): purl.

Pocket ribbing (RS): k13 (17, 21, 25), p1, *k1, p1*, rep from * 8 more times, k6, *p1, k1*, rep from * twice more.

Next row (WS): purl. Rep the last 2 rows 3 more times.

Next row (RS): k13 (17, 21, 25), bind off next 19 sts, work in pat to end.

Next row (WS): p12, purl across 19 sts from pocket stitch holder, p to end.

Resume working pat as follows, making decs as before until you have 41 (45, 49, 53) sts remaining (6 sts decreased):

RS rows: k to last 6 sts, *p1, k1*, rep from * twice more.

WS rows: purl.

Work even (no decs) until piece measures 17½" from bottom edge, ending with RS facing for next row.

TEENS' VERSION – 12 (14, 16)

Begin working pat as follows:

RS rows: k to last 6 sts, *p1, k1*, rep from * twice more.

WS rows: purl.

Rep the last 2 rows; until piece measures 6½ (7, 7½)" from bottom edge, ending with RS facing for next row.

BOTH VERSIONS

Armhole shaping: continuing in pat, bind off sts at beginning of RS rows only in the following sequence: bind off 3 sts once, then bind off 2 sts once, then bind off 1 st 3 times. You should have bound off a total of 8 sts at side-seam edge of the piece, to 21 (25, 29, 33, 37, 41, 47) sts remaining.

Continue in pat until piece measures 13½ (14½, 15½, 26, 26½, 27, 27½)" from bottom edge, ending with RS facing for next row.

Shoulder shaping: continuing in pat, bind off sts at beg of RS rows only in the following sequence: bind off 4 (5, 7, 7, 8, 9, 9) sts once, bind off 3 (4, 5, 6, 7, 7, 8) sts twice. Leave remaining 11 (12, 12, 14, 15, 18, 22) sts for neck on a spare needle or holder.

RIGHT FRONT

In brief, you will work Right Front as a mirror image of Left Front, making your armhole shaping and shoulder shaping at the beginning of the WS rows. Detailed instructions are as follows:

With larger needles, cast on 29 (33, 37, 47, 51, 55, 59) sts.

Work 12 rows of ribbing as given for Gauge Swatch.

WOMEN'S VERSION – SM (MD, LG, XL)

Begin working pat as follows:

RS rows: *k1, p1*, rep from * twice more, k to end of row.

WS rows: purl.

Rep the last 2 rows; AT THE SAME TIME, shaping side seam (left-hand edge on RS) on 13th row, and every 12th row thereafter as follows: *k1, p1*, rep from * twice more, k to last 3 sts, k2tog, k1.

Continue in pat as established until you have 44 (48, 52, 56) sts.

Next row (WS): purl.

Pocket ribbing: *k1, p1*, rep from * twice more, k6, p1, *k1, p1*, rep 8 more times, k to end.

Next row (WS): purl. Rep the last 2 rows 3 more times.

Next row (RS): *k1, p1*, rep from * twice more, k6, bind off next 19 sts, k to end.

Next row (WS): p13 (17, 21, 25), purl across 19 sts from pocket stitch holder, p to end.

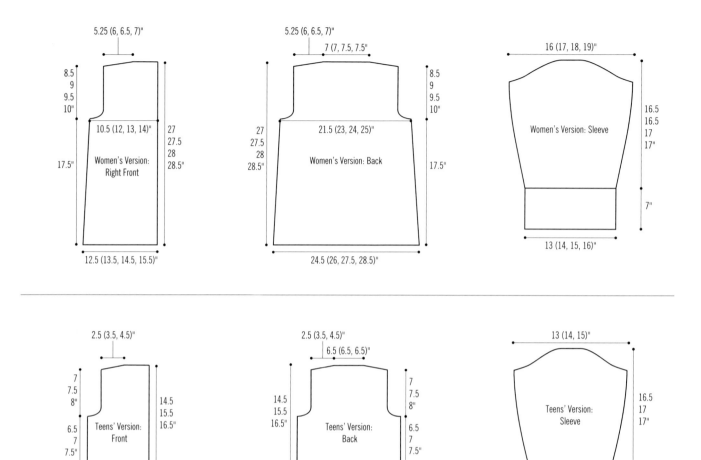

Women's Version: Right Front
- 5.25 (6, 6.5, 7)"
- 8.5, 9, 9.5, 10"
- 10.5 (12, 13, 14)"
- 27, 27.5, 28, 28.5"
- 17.5"
- 12.5 (13.5, 14.5, 15.5)"

Women's Version: Back
- 5.25 (6, 6.5, 7)"
- 7 (7, 7.5, 7.5)"
- 8.5, 9, 9.5, 10"
- 27, 27.5, 28, 28.5"
- 21.5 (23, 24, 25)"
- 17.5"
- 24.5 (26, 27.5, 28.5)"

Women's Version: Sleeve
- 16 (17, 18, 19)"
- 16.5, 16.5, 17, 17"
- 7"
- 13 (14, 15, 16)"

Teens' Version: Front
- 2.5 (3.5, 4.5)"
- 7, 7.5, 8"
- 6.5, 7, 7.5"
- 14.5, 15.5, 16.5"
- 8 (9, 10)"

Teens' Version: Back
- 2.5 (3.5, 4.5)"
- 6.5 (6.5, 6.5)"
- 14.5, 15.5, 16.5"
- 7, 7.5, 8"
- 6.5, 7, 7.5"
- 16 (18, 20)"

Teens' Version: Sleeve
- 13 (14, 15)"
- 16.5, 17, 17"
- 2"
- 11 (11.5, 12)"

Resume working pat as follows, making decs as before until you have 41 (45, 49, 53) sts remaining (6 sts decreased):

RS rows: *k1, p1*, rep from * twice more, k to end.

WS rows: purl.

Work even (no decs) until piece measures 17½" from bottom edge, ending with WS facing for next row.

TEENS' VERSION – 12 (14, 16)

Begin working pat as follows:

RS rows: *k1, p1*, rep from * twice more, k to end of row.

WS rows: purl.

Rep the last 2 rows; until piece measures 6½ (7, 7½)" from bottom edge, ending with WS facing for next row.

BOTH VERSIONS

Armhole shaping: continuing in pat, bind off sts at beginning of WS rows only in the following sequence: bind off 3 sts once, then bind off 2 sts once, then bind off 1 st 3 times. You should have bound off a total of 8 sts at side-seam edge of the piece, to 21 (25, 29, 33, 37, 41, 47) sts remaining.

Continue in pat until piece measures 13½ (14½, 15½, 26, 26½, 27, 27½)" from bottom edge, ending with WS facing for next row.

Shoulder shaping: continuing in pat, bind off sts at beginning of WS rows only in the following sequence: bind off 4 (5, 7, 7, 8, 9, 9) sts once, bind off 3 (4, 5, 6, 7, 7, 8) sts twice. Leave remaining 11 (12, 12, 14, 15, 18, 22) sts for neck on a spare needle or holder.

SLEEVES

With larger needles, cast on 41 (43, 45, 49, 53, 57, 61) sts.

Work ribbing as given for Gauge Swatch until piece measures 2 (2, 2, 7, 7, 7, 7)" from bottom edge, ending with RS facing for next row.

Begin working st st, making 1 inc at each side on 11th row, then every 10 rows thereafter, to 49 (53, 57, 61, 65, 69, 71) sts.

Work until even piece measures 13 (13, 13, 13, 13, 13½, 13½)" from beginning of st st, ending with RS facing for next row.

Sleeve cap shaping: continuing in st st, bind off sts at beginning of each row in the following sequence: bind off 5 (5, 5, 5, 6, 7, 8) sts once per side, then bind off 4 sts once per side, then bind off 3 sts 1 (1, 2, 2, 2, 2, 2) time(s) per side, bind off 2 sts once per side, bind off 1 st 4 (5, 4, 5, 5, 5, 5) times per side, bind off 2 sts twice per side. Bind off remaining 5 (7, 7, 9, 11, 13, 13) sts.

FINISHING

Do not block. Sew shoulder seams.

Collar: with RS of garment facing, purl across 11 (12, 12, 14, 15, 18, 22) sts from Right Front stitch holder, purl across 25 (25, 25, 27, 27, 29, 29) sts from Back neck holder, purl across 11 (12, 12, 14, 15, 18, 22) sts from Left Front holder, for a total of 47 (49, 49, 55, 57, 65, 73) sts.

Next row (WS of garment, but will be RS of collar when folded): *k1, p1*, rep from * twice more, k16 (17, 17, 20, 21, 25, 29), triple dec, k to last 6 sts, *p1, k1*, rep from * to end.

Next row (RS): purl.

Next row (WS): *k1, p1*, rep from * twice more, k15 (16, 16, 19, 20, 24, 28), triple dec, k to last 6 sts, *p1, k1*, rep from * to end.

Next row (RS): purl.

Next row (WS): *k1, p1*, rep from * twice more, k14 (15, 15, 18, 19, 23, 27), triple dec, k to last 6 sts, *p1, k1*, rep from * to end.

Next row (RS): purl.

Begin collar point shaping (WS): *k1, p1*, rep from * twice more, inc 1, k to last 7 sts, inc 1, *p1, k1*, rep from * to end.

Next row (RS): purl. Rep last 2 rows until you have 75 (77, 77, 83, 85, 93, 101) sts, ending with WS of garment facing for next row. Work 8 rows of ribbing as follows:

WS rows: k1, *p1, k1*, rep from * to end.

RS rows: purl.

Bind off loosely in pat.

WOMEN'S VERSION

Sew sleeve seams, reversing seams at cuff for fold-back. Sew side seams. Matching sleeve seams to side seams, sew sleeves to armholes. With WS facing, sew pocket edges to fronts.

Belt (for Women's version only): with smaller needles, cast on 9 sts.

RS rows: k1, *p1, k1*, rep from * to end of row.

WS rows: p1, *k1, p1*, rep from * to end of row. Rep the last 2 rows until belt measures 53 (56, 58, 60)" long. Bind off in pat.

Belt loops (make 2, for Women's version only): with smaller needles, cast on 12 sts. Knit 1 row.

Next row: bind off all sts. Fold in half to form loop and sew in place at side seam of garment.

TEENS' VERSION

Sew sleeve seams. Sew side seams. Matching sleeve seams to side seams, sew sleeves to armholes. 🍁

salish coat and hat

The Salish native Indians of North America's West Coast established a tradition of weaving blankets
for ceremonial wear and for their famous potlatch gatherings. I found one such blanket
with a dazzling array of patterns, given coherence with a recurring diamond motif at the side edges.
This coat picks up that unusual treatment along its asymmetrical front opening, which
when worn open, reveals the same pattern along the inner edge. In a mixture of lofty bouclé and
merino wool yarns, this coat is warm, yet lightweight.

SKILL LEVEL: EXPERIENCED

MEASUREMENTS

SIZES (in inches)	WOMEN			
	SM	MD	LG	XL
Finished Chest	41	46	49	52
Finished Length	28	28½	29	29½

MATERIALS

Yarn: Colors MC (Main Color), A, B: Indiecita Alpaca Bouclé
87% Alpaca, 13% Nylon (115 yds or 106 m/50 gr ball).
Colors C, D: Patons Classic Merino 100% Wool (221 yds or
204 m/100 gr ball). *See also page 126 for yarn information.*

NO. OF BALLS	WOMEN			
	SM	MD	LG	XL
MC: Black #109	6	7	7	8
A: Red #111	6	7	8	8
B: Gold #110	3	4	5	5
C: Loden #205	2	2	2	3
D: Blueberry #213	2	2	2	3

Needles: 1 pr. U.S. size 7 (4.5 mm) needles OR SIZE TO
OBTAIN GAUGE

Spare needle or st holder

Four 1" shank buttons and three ½" sew-through buttons

GAUGE

20 sts and 24 rows = 4" in st st

To work Gauge Swatch: with MC, cast on 24 sts and work st st
until piece measures 4" from bottom edge. Change to C and work
st st for another 4". Bind off. Block swatch by laying flat and
applying lots of steam with steam iron held just above the
swatch. Let cool and dry. If you have too many sts and rows to
the inch, switch to a larger needle; too few means you should
use a smaller needle.

*Your garment will not fit properly if the tension gauge is
incorrect! Take the time to check by making gauge swatch.*

*Directions are given for Women's size Small. Sizes Medium,
Large, and Extra-Large are given in parentheses. Where there
is only one number, it applies to all sizes.*

LEFT FRONT

With A, cast on 78 (82, 86, 90) sts. Work ribbing (*k1, p1*,
rep from * to end) in the following stripe sequence: *work 2
rows in A, then 2 rows in MC, rep from * once more, and inc
1 st at center of last row, to 79 (83, 87, 91) sts.

Work Chart I to end of chart, thus ending with RS facing for
next row. Note that the 10-row rep as marked is repeated
5 times in total. (See page 123 for tips on intarsia knitting.)

Work vertical stripes and Charts IV and V in intarsia st st,
establishing color placement as follows: with A, k21 (25, 24,
25); with D, k12 (13, 15, 16); with B, k20 (19, 22, 24),
work Row 7 of Chart IV, work Row 7 of Chart V.

Continue in st st, with stripe placement as established and
working to last row of Charts IV and V, then repeating chart
Rows 1 through 10, until piece measures 19½ (19¼, 19¼,
19)" from bottom edge, ending with RS facing for next row.

MC

A

B

C

D

Chart I

Work these
10 rows
5 times total

61   51   41   31   21   11

XL
(Start
RS rows
here)

LG
(Start
RS rows
here)

MD
(Start
RS rows
here)

SM
(Start
RS rows
here)

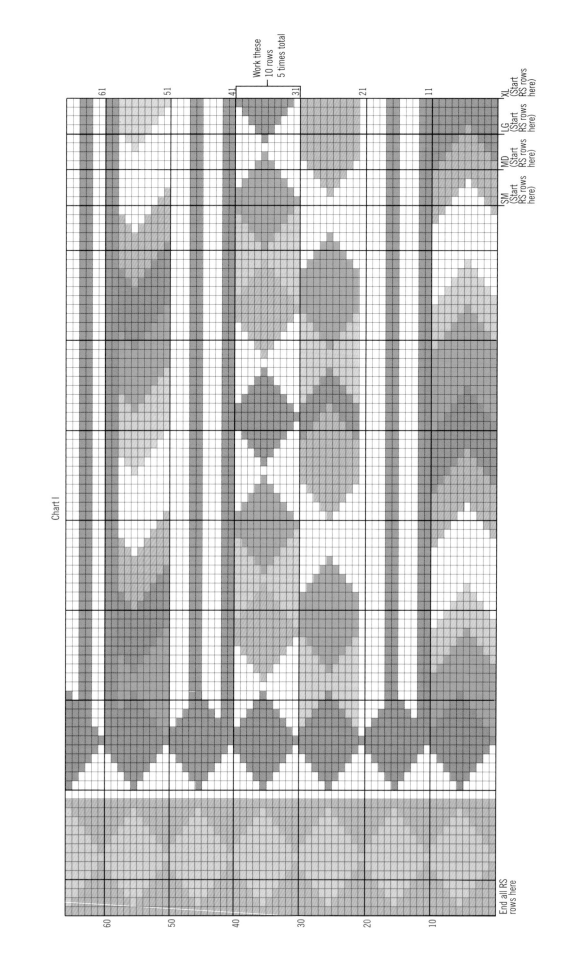

60   50   40   30   20   10

End all RS
rows here

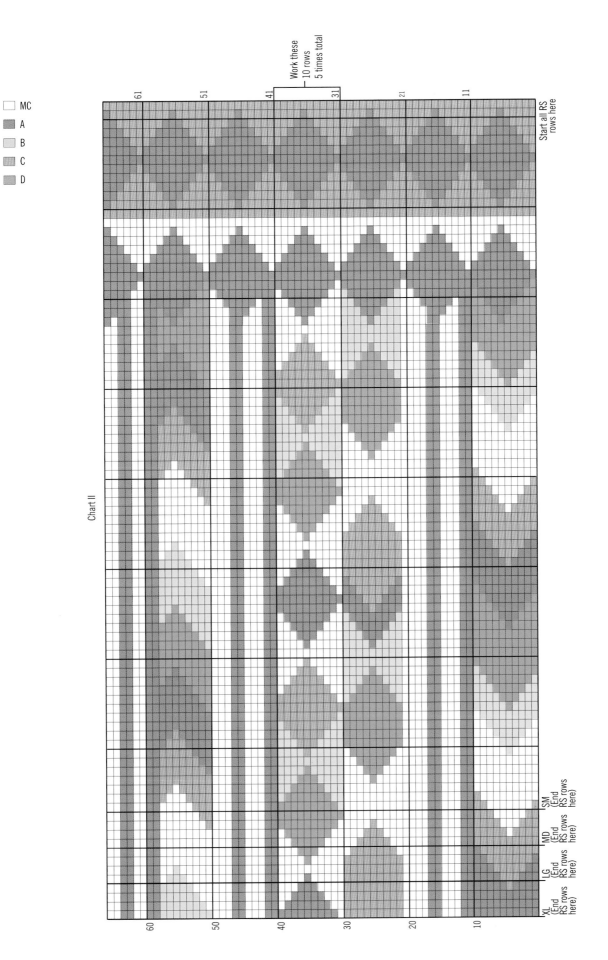

Chart II

MC
A
B
C
D

Work these 10 rows 5 times total

Start all RS rows here

61 · 51 · 41 · 31 · 21 · 11

SM (End RS rows here)
MD (End RS rows here)
LG (End RS rows here)
XL (End RS rows here)

60 · 50 · 40 · 30 · 20 · 10

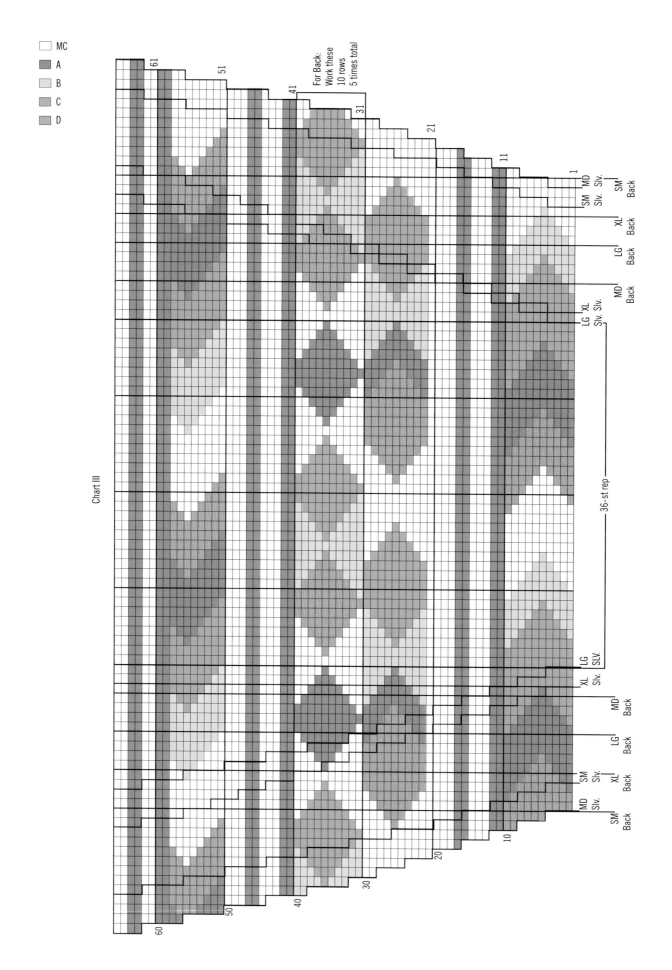

Chart III

MC
A
B
C
D

For Back:
Work these
10 rows
5 times total

36-st rep

Chart IV

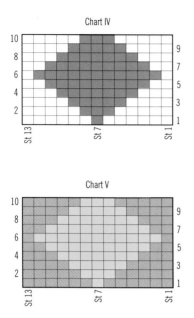

Chart V

Armhole shaping: bind off 9 (12, 9, 9) sts at beginning of next row. You should now have 70 (71, 78, 82) sts remaining. Continue even in intarsia pat until piece measures 8½ (9¼, 9¾, 10½)" from beginning of armhole shaping, ending with RS facing for next row.

Shoulder shaping and neckband: bind off 24 (26, 31, 35) sts for shoulder at beginning of next row. Work even on remaining 46 (45, 47, 47) sts until piece measures as close as possible to 1" from shoulder bind offs while ending with Row 10 of Charts IV and V and RS facing for next row. Using separate ball of C, cast on 33 (33, 39, 39) sts to spare needle and set aside for facing.

Next row (RS): with MC, cast on 13 (14, 18, 18) sts to end of left-hand needle. Starting with these cast-on sts and beginning with st #7 (7, 1, 1) of Chart IV, work to end of Row 1, then work full row of Chart IV 3 times across row. You should thus have 3½ (3½, 4, 4) diamond motifs for collar. Continue Row 1 with B and C: work full row of Chart V 3 times across row, end with sts #1 through #7 (7, 13, 13); AT THE SAME TIME, when you have worked to end of sts on left-hand needle, work across the 33 (33, 39, 39) sts cast on to the spare needle. You should thus have 3½ (3½, 4, 4) diamond motifs for facing, and you should now have 92 (92, 104, 104) sts across row.

Work to last row of Charts IV and V with placement as established, then work Row 1 once more.

Next row (WS): with C, p46 (46, 52, 52); with MC, p46 (46, 52, 52).

Next row (RS): bind off in pat.

RIGHT FRONT

With A, cast on 78 (82, 86, 90) sts. Work ribbing (*p1, k1*, rep from * to end) in the following stripe sequence: *work 2 rows in A, then 2 rows in MC, then rep from * once more, and inc 1 st at center of last row, to 79 (83, 87, 91) sts.

Work Chart II to end of chart, thus ending with RS facing for next row. Note that the 10-row rep as marked is repeated 5 times in total.

Work Charts IV and V and vertical stripes in intarsia st st, establishing placement as follows: work 1st 13 sts using Row 7 of Chart V, work next 13 sts using Row 7 of Chart IV, with A, k20 (19 22, 24); with D, k12 (13, 15, 16); with B, k21 (25, 24, 25).

Continue in st st with stripe placement as established and working to last row of Charts IV and V, then repeating chart Rows 1 through 10, until piece measures 19½ (19¼, 19¼, 19)" from bottom edge, ending with WS facing for next row.

Armhole shaping: bind off 9 (12, 9, 9) sts at beginning of next row. You should now have 70 (71, 78, 82) sts remaining. Continue even in intarsia pat until piece measures 8½ (9¼, 9¾, 10½)" from beginning of armhole shaping, ending with WS facing for next row.

Shoulder shaping and neckband: bind off 24 (26, 31, 35) sts for shoulder at beginning of next row. Work even on remaining 46 (45, 47, 47) sts until piece measures as close as possible to 1" from shoulder bind offs while ending with Row 10 of Charts IV and V, thus ending with RS facing for next row. Using separate ball of MC, cast on 13 (14, 18, 18) sts to spare needle and set aside.

Next row (RS): with C, cast on 33 (33, 39, 39) sts for facing at beginning of next row. Starting at st #7 (7, 1, 1), work Row 1 of Chart V, then work full row of Chart V 3 times across row. You should thus have 3½ (3½, 4, 4) diamond motifs for facing.

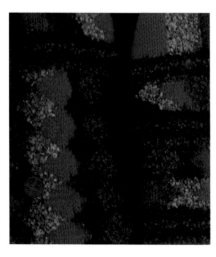

Continue Row 1 with MC and A: work full row of Chart IV 3 times across row, end with sts #1 through #7 (7, 13, 13); AT THE SAME TIME, when you have worked to end of sts on left-hand needle, work across sts on spare needle. You should thus have 3½ (3½, 4, 4) diamonds for collar, and you should now have 92 (92, 104, 104) sts across row.

Work to last row of charts with placement as established, then work Row 1 once more.

Next row (WS): with MC, p46 (46, 52, 52); with C, p46 (46, 52, 52).

Next row (RS): bind off in pat.

BACK

With A, cast on 102 (114, 122, 130) sts. Work k1, p1 ribbing as given for Left Front and inc 0 (1, 1, 0) st at center of last row, to 102 (115, 123, 130) sts.

Work Chart III. Note that the 36-st rep at center of chart is worked 2 (3, 3, 3) times, with additional sts at beginning and end of each row as shown. Work to end of chart, thus ending with RS facing for next row.

Work vertical stripes in intarsia st st, establishing color placement as follows: with B, k21 (25, 24, 25); with D, k12 (13, 15, 16); with A, k12 (13, 15, 16); with C, k12 (13, 15, 16); with B, k12 (13, 15, 16); with D, k12 (13, 15, 16); with A, k21 (25, 24, 25).

Continue in st st, with color placement as established, until piece measures 19½ (19¼, 19¼, 19)" from bottom edge, ending with RS facing for next row.

Armhole shaping: bind off 9 (12, 9, 9) sts at beginning of each of the next 2 rows. You should now have 84 (91, 105, 112) sts remaining. Continue even in intarsia pat until piece measures 8½ (9¼, 9¾, 10½)" from beginning of armhole shaping, ending with RS facing for next row.

Shoulder shaping and neckband: bind off 24 (26, 31, 35) sts at beginning of next 2 rows. Work even on remaining 36 (39, 43, 42) sts for Back neck until piece matches length of Front to beginning of neckband, ending with RS facing for next row. Bind off in pat.

SLEEVES

With A, cast on 60 (64, 72, 74) sts. Worked striped (k1, p1) ribbing as given for Left Front and inc 0 (1, 0, 1) st at center of last row, to 60 (65, 72, 75) sts.

Work Chart III. Note that the 36-st rep at center of chart is worked 1 (1, 2, 2) time(s), with additional sts at beginning and end of each row as shown, and sides are shaped with increases as shown. Work to end of chart, thus ending with RS facing for next row. You should now have 84 (91, 98, 105) sts.

Work even (no further incs) in vertically striped st st, establishing color placement as follows: with B, k12 (13, 14, 15); with D, k12 (13, 14, 15); with A, k12 (13, 14, 15); with C, k12 (13, 14, 15); with B, k12 (13, 14, 15); with D, k12 (13, 14, 15); with A, k12 (13, 14, 15).

Continue in st st, with color placement as established, until piece measures 20 (20½, 20½, 20½)" from bottom edge, ending with RS facing for next row. Bind off in pat.

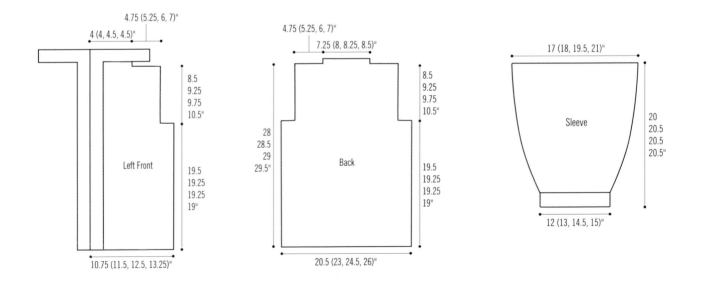

Block pieces to measurements. Sew shoulder seams. With right sides together, sew short vertical edges of neckband extensions (in MC and A) together, then placing this seam at center of Back neck edge, sew the bottom edge of extensions to Back neck edge. Sew short vertical edges of neckband facings (in B and C) together. With right sides together fold facings to inside along fold lines indicated on measurement diagram. Matching center back seams of neckbands together, sew upper edges of facing and neckband together. *Hint: for a crisp edge at top fold, sew only through WS loops of cast-off sts (rather than both loops as usual). Thus when collar is folded right side out, the RS loops of cast-off sts are showing, making a crisp edge.*

Button loops (make 4): with MC, cast on 12 sts, leaving a long tail. Knit 1 row, then bind off all sts, leaving a long tail. Using the tails, sew loops at facing fold line, positioning 1 loop at collar, and the rest as shown in photo.

Fold facings right side out, and with WS facing you, stitch facings in place on inner garment.

Sew sleeve top to vertical armhole edges. Sew upper section of sleeve underarm seam to armhole bound-off sts. Sew side seams and remaining sleeve seams together.

Sew buttons to correspond to button loops. To prevent the 3 lower buttons from pulling the fabric, place small sew-through button on WS of garment behind large button and sew through both buttons to join.

HAT

Crown: with A, cast on 100 sts. Work in st st until piece measures 5½" from bottom edge, ending with RS facing for next row.

Next row (RS): purl.

Next row (WS): knit.

SHAPE CROWN

Row 1 (RS): *k2tog, k8*, rep from * to end of row.

Row 2 (WS): purl.

Row 3 (RS): *k2tog, k7*, rep from * to end of row.

Row 4 (WS): purl.

Continue in this manner, decreasing 10 sts every RS row (working one less st between decs on every following RS row), until you have 10 sts remaining.

Next row (WS): p2tog 5 times, to 5 sts. Break yarn, leaving a long tail, and draw through remaining sts to fasten.

Brim: with MC, cast on 26 sts.

Row 1 (RS): k2, work Row 1 of Chart IV, yo, k2tog, k9.

Row 2 (WS): p11, work Row 2 of Chart IV, p2.

Row 3 (RS): k2, work Row 3 of Chart IV, yo, k2tog, k9.

Row 4 (WS): p11, work Row 4 of Chart IV, p2.

Charted pat is now in position; continue in pat as established until you have completed 12 diamonds. Bind off.

Finishing: sew crown seam. Sew short edges of brim together. Fold brim along fold line created with yo's. Pin bottom edge of crown in place between 2 layers of brim and sew through all 3 layers to fasten, making sure that diamonds will show when brim is folded up. ❧

gryphon

Like all designers, certain motifs and epochs in decorative art have special resonance for me. I return to medieval paintings and textiles again and again, especially those of Great Britain. This intarsia gryphon (or "griffin") was the fantastical half bird, half beast of the Dark Ages' imaginings, here contained by borders of Fair Isle quatrefoils and stained-glass motifs.

SKILL LEVEL: EXPERIENCED

MEASUREMENTS

SIZES (in inches)	ADULTS			
	SM	MD	LG	XL
Finished Chest	43	46	51	53½
Finished Length	26	26½	27	27½

MATERIALS

Yarn: Naturally Café 42% Wool, 28% Alpaca, 26% Mohair, 4% Nylon (83 yds or 77 m/50 gr ball). *See also page 126 for yarn information.*

NO. OF BALLS	ADULTS			
	SM	MD	LG	XL
MC: Petrol Blue #716	8	9	9	10
A: Aubergine #717	5	6	6	7
B: Copper #714	7	8	8	9

Needles: 1 pr. each U.S. sizes 6 and 7 (4 mm and 4.5 mm) needles OR SIZE TO OBTAIN GAUGE

Spare needle or stitch holder

GAUGE

19 sts and 20 rows = 4" in st st using larger needles

19 sts and 22 rows = 4" in Chart I pat using larger needles

To work Gauge Swatch: with MC and larger needles, cast on 25 sts and work st st (k all sts on RS and p all sts on WS) until piece measures 4" from bottom edge. Work Row 1 of Chart I, working 6-st rep 4 times across row, then working st #7 at end, reading chart from right to left. Work Row 2 of chart: work st #7, then work 6-st rep 4 times across row, reading chart from left to right. Continue working through rows of chart, reading RS rows from right to left and WS rows from left to right, and carrying out-of-work color across the WS of work. Bind off. Block swatch by laying flat and applying lots of steam with steam iron held just above the swatch. Let cool and dry. If you have too many sts and rows to the inch, switch to a larger needle; too few means you should use a smaller needle. (You may find you need to use a larger needle for the charted pat than you need for the st st.)

Your garment will not fit properly if the tension gauge is incorrect! Take the time to check by making gauge swatch.

Directions are given for Adults' size Small. Sizes Medium, Large, and Extra-Large are given in parentheses. Where there is only one number, it applies to all sizes.

FRONT

With B and smaller needles, cast on 103 (109, 121, 127) sts.

Next row (RS): with B, purl.

Work striped ribbing as follows, carrying out-of-work color across the WS of work:

Row 1 (WS): with B, k1. *With A, p2. With B, k1.* Rep from * to end.

Row 2 (RS): with B, p1. *With A, k2. With B, p1.* Rep from * to end.

Rows 3 through 5: rep the last 2 rows once more, then work Row 1 once more.

With B, knit 2 rows.

MC

A

B

B (k on WS)

Chart I

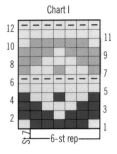

Chart II

Chart = 55 sts wide

Chart III

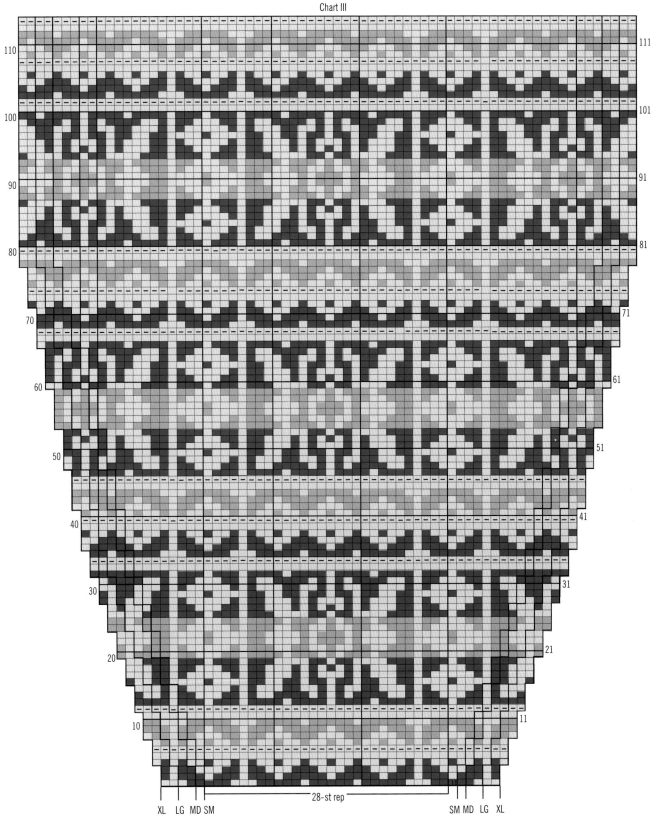

Change to larger needles and begin Chart I, establishing placement as follows:

Row 1 (RS): work 6-st rep 17 (18, 20, 21) times across row, reading chart from right to left, then work st #7.

Row 2 (WS): work st #7, then purl 6-st rep to end, reading chart from left to right. Chart is now in position. Work Rows 3 through 6 of Chart I (noting that Row 6 is knitted), thus ending with RS facing for next row.

Proceed in st st as follows, twisting colors on WS to join: with MC, k68 (72, 80, 84), with A, k to end.

Next row (WS): with A, p 35 (37, 41, 43); with MC, p to end. Rep the last 2 rows until piece measures 3½ (3½, 4, 4½)" from bottom edge, ending with RS facing for next row.

Begin Chart II, placing chart as follows: with MC, k38 (42, 50, 54). Work Row 1 of chart, switching background color to A at same position as established, and carrying 1 ball of B across WS while working areas between feet and legs. Work A to end.

Chart II is now in position; continue working through rows of chart with placement as established until chart is complete. AT THE SAME TIME, when piece measures 17" from bottom edge, ending with RS facing for next row, work armhole shaping as follows:

Armhole shaping: bind off 3 (4, 4, 3) sts at beginning of each of the next 2 rows. You should now have 97 (101, 113, 121) sts remaining. Hereafter, position chart as follows (RS): with MC, k35 (38, 46, 51), work next 55 sts in chart as established; with A, k to end.

When Chart II is complete, resume working st st in A and MC as before, until piece measures 24 (24½, 25, 25½)" from bottom edge, ending with RS facing for next row. With B, knit 2 rows, thus ending with RS facing for next row.

Left side neck shaping:
Next row (RS): work 43 (43, 49, 55) sts in Row 1 of Chart I, working 6-st rep 7 (7, 8, 9) times across and ending with st #7 of chart. Turn, leaving remaining sts on a spare needle.

Continue working through rows of Chart I as established; AT THE SAME TIME, shape neck as follows:

Row 1 (WS): bind off 4 (5, 5, 6) sts, work to end in charted pat.

Row 2 (RS): work in charted pat to last 2 sts, p2tog.

Row 3 (WS): bind off 3 (3, 3, 4) sts, work to end in charted pat.

Row 4 (RS): rep Row 2.

Row 5 (WS): bind off 1 st, work to end in charted pat. Rep the last 2 rows until you have 30 (30, 34, 38) sts remaining for shoulder. Left side neck shaping is complete.

Continue working through rows of Chart I until chart is complete, thus ending with RS facing for next row.

Next row (RS): with B, bind off.

Right side neck shaping: with RS facing, join B to sts on spare needle. With B, bind off 11 (15, 15, 11) sts, then work Row 1 of Chart I (including st remaining from bind offs), working 6-st rep 7 (7, 8, 9) times across and ending with st #7 of chart.

Continue working through rows of Chart I as established; AT THE SAME TIME, shape neck as follows:

Row 1 (WS): work in charted pat to last 2 sts, p2tog.

Row 2 (RS): bind off 4 (5, 5, 6) sts, work to end in charted pat.

Row 3 (WS): rep Row 1.

Row 4 (RS): bind off 3 (3, 3, 4) sts, work to end in charted pat.

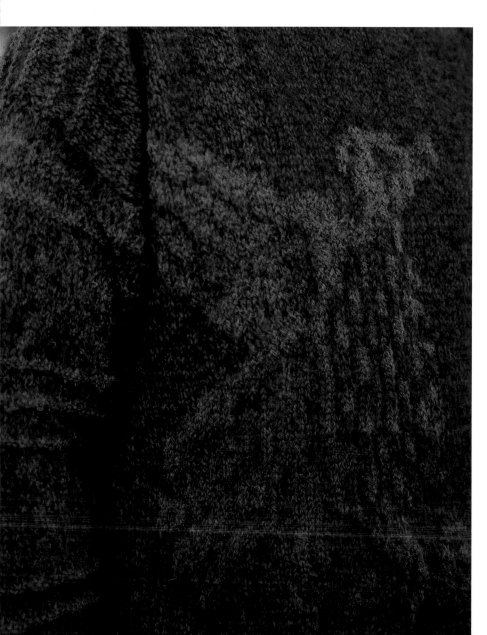

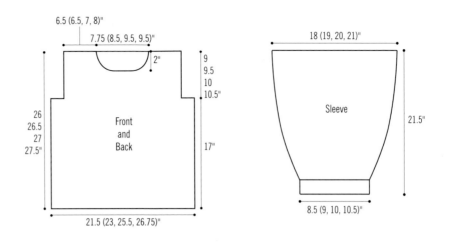

QUICK TIP: *When you're picking up collar stitches around a neck edge, first find and mark the center back and center front points with a scrap of contrast yarn or safety pin — this makes it easier to divide your stitches evenly on each side.*

Row 5 (WS): rep Row 1.

Row 6 (RS): bind off 1 st, work to end in charted pat. Rep the last 2 rows until you have 30 (30, 34, 38) sts remaining for shoulder. Right side neck shaping is complete.

Continue working through rows of chart until chart is complete, thus ending with RS facing for next row.

Next row (RS): with B, bind off.

BACK

With smaller needles and B, cast on 103 (109, 121, 127) sts as for Front and purl 1 row. Work 5 rows striped ribbing as for Front. With B, knit 2 rows.

Change to larger needles and work Rows 1 through 6 of Chart I as given for Front.

Proceed in st st as follows, twisting colors on WS to join: with A, k35 (37, 41, 43); with MC, k to end.

Next row (WS): with MC, p68 (72, 80, 84); with A, p to end.

Rep the last 2 rows until piece measures 17" from bottom edge. Work armhole shaping as for Front.

Continue working even in st st as established until piece measures 24 (24½, 25, 25½)" from bottom edge, ending with RS facing for next row.

With B, knit the next 2 rows and inc 0 (2, 2, 0) sts evenly across 2nd row, to 97 (103, 115, 121) sts.

Next row (RS): work Row 1 of Chart I, working 6-st rep 16 (17, 19, 20) times across and ending with st #7 of chart.

Continue working through rows of Chart I until chart is complete, thus ending with RS facing for next row.

Next row (RS): with B, bind off.

SLEEVES

With smaller needles and B, cast on 43 (46, 49, 52) sts and purl 1 row.

Work 5 rows striped ribbing as given for Front.

With B, knit 2 rows and inc 14 (13, 14, 15) sts evenly across 2nd row, to 57 (59, 63, 67) sts.

Next row (RS): change to larger needles and begin Chart III, noting that 28-st rep is worked twice, with additional sts at beginning and end of each row as shown. Work through rows of Chart III, making incs at side seam as shown, until chart is complete.

Next row (RS): with B, bind off.

FINISHING

Sew right shoulder seam, matching charted motifs at Front and Back shoulders.

Collar: with RS facing, using smaller needles, and B, pick up and knit 24 (26, 27, 27) sts along left Front neck edge, 24 (26, 27, 27) sts along right Front neck edge, and 37 (39, 43, 43) sts along Back neck edge, for a total of 85 (91, 97, 97) sts.

Row 1 (WS): with B, purl.

Begin Chart I, establishing placement as follows:

Row 2 (RS): work 6-st rep 14 (15, 16, 16) times across row, reading chart from right to left, then work st #7. Work Rows 2 through 6 of Chart I, thus ending with RS facing for next row.

Work striped Fair Isle ribbing as follows:

Row 1 (RS): with B, p1. *With A, k2. With B, p1.* Rep from * to end.

Row 2 (WS): with B, k1. *With A, p2. With B, k1.* Rep from * to end.

Rep the last 2 rows once more. With B, knit 2 rows.

Next row (RS): with B, bind off.

Sew collar seam and left shoulder seam, matching charted motifs at Front and Back shoulders. Sew sleeve cap to vertical armhole edges. Sew upper section of sleeve underarm seam to armhole bound-off sts. Sew remaining sleeve seams and side seams together. ❧

spring

heidi

Delicate alpine flowers and crystalline beads add to the prettiness of this three-quarter sleeved top with notched neckline. Shown here in mauve with pastels, this design would also be lovely with a fresh white background.

SKILL LEVEL: INTERMEDIATE

MEASUREMENTS

SIZES (in inches)	TEENS			WOMEN			
	12	14	16	SM	MD	LG	XL
Finished Chest	29	31	35	37½	39½	44	46
Finished Length	18	19	20	21	22	22½	23

MATERIALS

Yarn: Diamond's Cantata 100% Cotton Crepe DK (115 yds or 106 m/50 gr ball). *See also page 126 for yarn information.*

NO. OF BALLS	TEEN			WOMEN			
	12	14	16	SM	MD	LG	XL
MC: Mauve #9600	6	7	8	9	9	10	11
A: White #460	1	1	1	1	1	1	1
B: Buttercup #08	1	1	1	1	1	1	1
C: Periwinkle #2600	1	1	1	1	1	1	1
D: Willow #5690	1	1	1	1	1	1	1

Needles: 1 pr. each U.S. sizes 5 and 6 (3.5 mm and 4 mm) needles OR SIZE TO OBTAIN GAUGE

U.S. size 5 (3.5 mm) circular needle, 24" or 29" long

Spare needle or stitch holder

Seven 5 mm glass beads and six 2 mm silver beads

GAUGE

22 sts and 28 rows = 4" in st st and Fair Isle using larger needles

To work Gauge Swatch: with larger needles, cast on 25 sts and work seeded rib pat as follows:

Row 1 (RS): p1, *k2, p1*, rep from * to end of row.

Row 2 (WS): purl.

Rep the last 2 rows to form pat.

When piece measures 2" from bottom edge, begin chart (page 92) on next RS row, working 6-st rep 4 times across row, then end with st #1, reading RS rows of chart from right to left and WS rows from left to right. Carry out-of-work color loosely across WS of work. When swatch measures 4" from bottom edge, bind off. Block swatch by laying flat and applying lots of steam with steam iron held just above the swatch. Let cool and dry. If you have too many sts and rows to the inch, switch to a larger needle; too few means you should use a smaller needle. *Hint: you may need to use a larger needle for the Fair Isle sections to achieve consistent gauge and avoid distorting or pulling the knitted stitches.*

Your garment will not fit properly if the tension gauge is incorrect! Take the time to check by making gauge swatch.

Directions are given for Teens' size 12. Teens' sizes 14, 16, and Women's sizes Small, Medium, Large, and Extra-Large are given in parentheses. Where there is only one number, it applies to all sizes.

FRONT

With smaller needles and MC, cast on 79 (85, 97, 103, 109, 121, 127) sts.

Work ribbing:

Row 1 (RS): p1, *k2, p1*, rep from * to end of row.

Row 2 (WS): k1, *p2, k1*, rep from * to end of row.

Rep the last 2 rows once more.

Change to larger needles and begin seeded rib pat as given for Gauge Swatch; AT THE SAME TIME, dec 1 st at each side every 2nd row 3 (3, 3, 2, 2, 1, 1) time(s), then every 4th row 3 (3, 3, 4, 4, 5, 5) times. You should now have 67 (73, 85, 91, 97, 109, 115) sts.

Work even in pat, if necessary, until piece measures 3½ (3½, 3½, 4, 4, 4½, 4½)".

Continue in pat, and inc 1 at each side on next RS row, then every following 10th row 5 times, until you have 79 (85, 97, 103, 109, 121, 127) sts.

Work even, if necessary, until piece measures 12½ (13, 13½, 14, 14½, 14½, 14½)" from bottom edge, ending with RS facing for next row.

Armhole shaping: bind off sts at the beginning of each row as follows: bind off 3 (3, 4, 4, 4, 4, 4) sts 3 times. You should now have 61 (67, 73, 79, 85, 97, 103) sts.

Yoke (RS): work Row 1 of chart, reading chart from right to left and placing pat as follows: work 6-st rep 10 (11, 12, 13, 14, 16, 17) times across row, end with St #1. *(See page 123 for more information on Fair Isle knitting.)*

Next row (WS): work Row 2 of chart, reading chart from left to right and placing pat as follows: work St #1, then work 6-st rep 10 (11, 12, 13, 14, 16, 17) times across row. Continue working through rows of chart with placement as established until piece measures 1¾ (1¾, 2, 2¼, 2½, 3, 3½)" from beginning of armhole shaping, ending with RS facing for next row.

Left side keyhole opening: keeping continuity of pat, work 30 (33, 36, 39, 42, 48, 51) sts. Turn, leaving remaining sts on spare needle or holder.

Next row (WS): work in charted pat as established.

*Next row (RS): Work 1 row in pat.
Next row (WS): bind off 1 st, work to end of row in pat.* Rep from * 3 more times.

Continue even in pat until length measures 3½ (3½, 4, 4, 4½, 5, 5½)" from beginning of armhole shaping, ending with WS facing for next row.

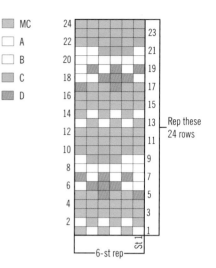

☐ MC		
☐ A		
☐ B		
☐ C		
☐ D		

Rep these 24 rows

6-st rep — St 1

Left side neck shaping: keeping continuity of pat, bind off sts at beginning of WS rows in the following sequence: bind off 6 sts once, bind off 4 sts twice, bind off 2 sts 1 (1, 1, 2, 3, 3, 3) time(s), bind off 1 st 2 (3, 3, 2, 2, 2, 3) times. You should now have 8 (10, 13, 15, 16, 22, 24) sts remaining for shoulder. Work even in pat until piece measures 5½ (6, 6½, 7, 7½, 8, 8½)" from beginning of armhole shaping, ending with RS facing for next row. Bind off.

Right side keyhole opening: with RS facing, join yarn (in colors to keep continuity of pat) to first st on spare needle; k2tog, work in pat to end of row.

*Next row (WS): work in charted pat as established.

Next row (RS): bind off 1 st, work to end of row in pat.* Rep from * 3 more times.

Continue even in pat until length measures 3½ (3½, 4, 4, 4½, 5, 5½)" from beginning of armhole shaping, ending with RS facing for next row.

Right side neck shaping: keeping continuity of pat, bind off sts at beginning of RS rows in the following sequence: bind off 6 sts once, bind off 4 sts twice, bind off 2 sts 1 (1, 1, 2, 3, 3, 3) time(s), bind off 1 st 2 (3, 3, 2, 2, 2, 3) times. You should now have 8 (10, 13, 15, 16, 22, 24) sts remaining for shoulder. Work even in pat until piece measures 5½ (6, 6½, 7, 7½, 8, 8½)" from beginning of armhole shaping, ending with RS facing for next row. Bind off.

BACK

Work as for Front, but omit keyhole opening and neck shaping: after completing armhole shaping, work even until length of piece matches length of Front to shoulder, ending with RS facing for next row. Bind off.

SLEEVES

With smaller needles and A, cast on 43 (49, 49, 52, 58, 61, 67) sts.

Change to MC and work 4 rows ribbing as given for Front.

Change to larger needles and work seeded rib pat as given for Gauge Swatch. Work remainder of sleeve in seeded rib pat using MC; AT THE SAME TIME, inc 1 st at each side every 6th row 1 (1, 2, 6, 6, 9, 8) time(s), then every 8th row 8 (8, 9, 6, 6, 4, 5) times, until you have 61 (67, 71, 76, 82, 87, 93) sts. Work your incs into seeded rib pat.

Work even in pat until piece measures 11½ (12½, 13, 13½, 13½, 13½, 14)" from bottom edge, ending with RS facing for next row.

Sleeve cap shaping: continuing in pat, bind off sts at the beginning of each row in the following sequence: bind off 4 sts 1 (2, 2, 3, 2, 4, 4) time(s); bind off 3 sts 2 (2, 3, 2, 3, 3, 3) times; bind off 2 sts 2 (2, 2, 2, 3, 2, 3) times; bind off 1 st 2 (1, 3, 2, 1, 1, 1) time(s); bind off 2 sts 1 (1, 1, 1, 2, 1, 1) time(s), bind off 3 sts 2 (2, 1, 1, 1, 1, 1) time(s).

Next Row (RS): bind off remaining 13 (13, 13, 18, 20, 17, 19) sts.

FINISHING

With RS facing, using MC and smaller needles, pick up and knit 11 sts along each side of keyhole opening. Work 1 row of ribbing as follows: *k1, p1* rep from * to end of row. With A, bind off in pat (bind off k sts knitwise and p sts purlwise).

Sew shoulder seams. With RS facing, using MC and circular needle, pick up and knit 23 (24, 24, 27, 29, 29, 30) sts along left Front neck edge, pick up and knit 41 (43, 43, 45, 49, 49, 51) sts along Back neck edge, pick up and knit 23 (24, 24, 27, 29, 29, 30) sts along right Front neck edge, for a total of 87 (91, 91, 99, 107, 107, 111) sts. Working back and forth on needle (do not join into round), work 1 row of ribbing as follows: p1, *k1, p1* rep from * to end of row. With A, bind off in pat. Thread a needle with a doubled strand of strong thread, then put beads (as shown in photo on facing page) onto needle. Sew end to other corner of keyhole to fasten. Sew sleeve seams and side seams. Sew in sleeves, matching center of sleeve caps to shoulder seams. ✦

QUICK TIP: *Keeping your place when using charts is easy if you use those ubiquitous sticky notes — and you can write reminders on the notes as you go.*

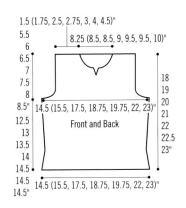

1.5 (1.75, 2.5, 2.75, 3, 4, 4.5)"
5.5
6
6.5
7
7.5
8
8.5"
12.5
13
13.5
14
14.5
14.5
14.5
8.25 (8.5, 8.5, 9, 9.5, 9.5, 10)"
18
19
20
21
22
22.5
23"
14.5 (15.5, 17.5, 18.75, 19.75, 22, 23)"
Front and Back
14.5 (15.5, 17.5, 18.75, 19.75, 22, 23)"

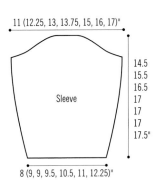

11 (12.25, 13, 13.75, 15, 16, 17)"
14.5
15.5
16.5
17
17
17
17.5"
Sleeve
8 (9, 9, 9.5, 10.5, 11, 12.25)"

spring garden twinset

The same impulses that inspire a knitter also inspire a gardener: creativity and the pleasure to be derived from working with one's hands immersed in color and texture. This cardigan's embossed flowers, worked in twist stitches, grow from a seed-stitch border. Underneath is a simple matching shell.

CARDIGAN SKILL LEVEL: EXPERIENCED, SHELL SKILL LEVEL: VERY EASY

MEASUREMENTS

SIZES (in inches)		WOMEN		
	SM	MD	LG	XL
Cardigan Finished Chest	37½	40	44	46½
Cardigan Finished Length	20	20½	21	21½
Shell Finished Chest	35	37	40½	43
Shell Finished Length	16½	17	17½	18

MATERIALS

Yarn: Estelle Designs Young Touch 100% Cotton DK (114 yds or 105 m/50 gr ball). *See also page 126 for yarn information.*

NO. OF BALLS		WOMEN		
	SM	MD	LG	XL
Cardigan, #75008 Buttercup	10	11	12	13
Shell, #75008 Buttercup	4	5	6	7

Needles: 1 pr. U.S. size 6 (4 mm) needles OR SIZE TO OBTAIN GAUGE

U.S. size 6 (4 mm) crochet hook for cardigan

Spare needle or stitch holder

Seven ³⁄₈" buttons

SPECIAL ABBREVIATIONS

RT = Right Twist: reverses the order in which the next 2 stitches are knit, twisting the sts to the right. **On RS rows:** with the yarn in back, ignore the next st on left needle and k the 2nd st through the front of the loop, do not slide off left needle, then k the first st (the previously ignored st) through back of loop, slip both sts from needle. **On WS rows:** with yarn at WS, p the 2nd st through the front of the loop (at WS), do not slide off left needle, then p the first st through front of loop (at WS), slip both sts from needle.

LT = Left Twist: reverses the order in which the next 2 stitches are knit, twisting the sts to the left. **On RS rows:** with the yarn in back, ignore the next st on left needle and k the 2nd st through back of loop, do not slide off left needle, bring the right needle around to the RS and k the first st (the previously ignored st) through front of loop, slide both sts from needle. **On WS rows:** with yarn at WS, p the 2nd st through the back of the loop (at RS), do not slide off left needle, then p the first st through front of loop (at WS), slip both sts from needle.

MB = Make Bobble: inc 1 in the next st, turn work, and inc 1 purlwise twice. Turn again and k4. Turn again and p2tog twice. Turn again and k2tog.

GAUGE

22 sts and 28 rows = 4" in reverse st st

To work Gauge Swatch: cast on 24 sts and work reverse st st (p all sts on RS and k all sts on WS) until piece measures 4" from bottom edge. Bind off. Block swatch by laying flat and applying lots of steam with steam iron held just above the swatch. Let cool and dry. If you have too many sts and rows to the inch, change to a larger needle; too few means you should use a smaller needle.

Your garment will not fit properly if the tension gauge is incorrect! Take the time to check by making gauge swatch.

Directions are given for Women's size Small. Women's sizes Medium, Large, and Extra-Large are given in parentheses. Where there is only one number, it applies to all sizes.

Note: you can work the twist-stitch motifs on the cardigan from either the charts on page 100 or the following written panel pats, placing the motifs as directed in the pattern on page 99.

PANEL PAT 1 (WORKED OVER 31 STS)

Rows 1 and 3 (RS): p8, k1, p14, k2, p6.

Rows 2 and 4 (WS): k6, p2, k14, p1, k8.

Row 5 (RS): p8, k1, p14, k1, LT, p5.

Row 6 (WS): k5, p1, k1, p1, k14, p1, k8.

Row 7 (RS): p8, k1, p13, RT, p1, LT, p4.

Row 8 (WS): k4, p1, k2, p2, k13, p1, k8.

Row 9 (RS): p7, RT, p12, RT, k1, p2, LT, p3.

Row 10 (WS): [k3, p1] twice, k1, p1 k13, p1, k7.

Row 11 (RS): p6, RT, p12, RT, p1, k1, p3, LT, p2.

Row 12 (WS): k2, p2, k3, p1, k2, p1, k13, p1, k6.

Row 13 (RS): p5, RT, p12, RT, p2, k1, p2, RT, LT, p1.

Row 14 (WS): k1, [p1, k2] 3 times, k1, p1, k13, p1, k5.

Row 15 (RS): p5, k1, p12, RT, p3, k1, p1, RT, p2, LT.

Row 16 (WS): p1, k4, p1, k1, p1, k3, p2, k12, p1, k5.

Row 17 (RS): p5, k1, p11, RT, LT, p2, k1, p1, LT, p2, RT.

Row 18 (WS): k1, [p1, k2] 4 times, p1, k11, p1, k5.

Row 19 (RS): p5, LT, p9, RT, p2, LT, p1, k1, p2, LT, RT, p1.

Row 20 (WS): k2, p2, k3, p1, k1, p1, k4, p1, k9, p2, k5.

Row 21 (RS): p4, RT, LT, p8, LT, p2, RT, p1, k1, p3, LT, p2.

Row 22 (WS): k7, p1, [k2, p1] twice, k9, p1, k2, p1, k4.

Row 23 (RS): p3, RT, p2, LT, p8, LT, RT, p1, RT, p7.

Row 24 (WS): k7, p2, k2, p2, k9, p1, k3, p2, k3.

Row 25 (RS): p2, RT, LT, p2, LT, p8, RT, p1, RT, LT, p6.

Row 26 (WS): k6, p2, k1, p1, k11, p1, k2, p2, k2, p1, k2.

Row 27 (RS): p1, RT, p2, LT, p2, k1, p10, RT, p1, k1, LT, p5.

Row 28 (WS): k5, p1, k1, p1, k2, p1, k10, p1, k2, p1, k4, p1, k1.

Row 29 (RS): p1, LT, p2, RT, p2, k1, p9, RT, p2, k1, p1, LT, p4.

Row 30 (WS): k4, p1, k2, p1, k3, p1, k9, p1, k3, [p1, k2] twice.

Row 31 (RS): p2, LT, RT, p2, RT, p8, RT, p3, k1, p2, LT, p3.

Row 32 (WS): [k3, p1] 3 times, p1, k8, p1, k4, p2, k3.

Row 33 (RS): p3, RT, p2, RT, LT, p6, RT, LT, p2, k1, p3, LT, p2.

Row 34 (WS): k2, p2, k3, [p1, k2] twice, p1, k6, p1, k2, p1, k7.

Row 35 (RS): p6, RT, p2, LT, p4, RT, p2, LT, p1, k1, p2, RT, LT, p1.

Row 36 (WS): k1, [p1, k2] twice, p1, k1, [p1, k4] twice, p2, k3, p1, k6.

Row 37 (RS): p5, RT, p2, RT, LT, p3, LT, p2, RT, p1, k1, p1, RT, p2, LT.

Row 38 (WS): p1, k4, p1, k1, [p1, k2] twice, p1, k4, p1, k2, p1, k3, p1, k5.

Row 39 (RS): p5, k1, p2, RT, p2, LT, p3, LT, RT, p2, k1, p1, LT, p2, RT.

Row 40 (WS): k1, [p1, k2] twice, p1, k3, p2, [k4, p1] twice, k2, p1, k5.

Row 41 (RS): p5, k1, p2, LT, p2, RT, p4, [RT, p2] twice, LT, RT, p1.

Row 42 (WS): k2, p2, k3, p2, k9, p1, k2, p1, k3, p1, k5.

Row 43 (RS): p5, LT, p2, LT, RT, p8, RT, k1, p3, LT, p2.

Row 44 (WS): k7, p1, k1, p1, k9, p2, k3, p2, k5.

Row 45 (RS): p4, RT, LT, p2, LT, p8, RT, p1, LT, p6.

Row 46 (WS): k6, p2, k2, p1, k12, p1, k2, p1, k4.

Row 47 (RS): p3, RT, p2, LT, p10, RT, p2, k1, LT, p5.

Row 48 (WS): k5, p1, k1, p1, k3, p1, k10, p1, k3, p2, k3.

Row 49 (RS): p2, RT, LT, p2, LT, p8, RT, p3, k1, p1, LT, p4.

Row 50 (WS): k4, p1, k2, p1, k3, p2, k8, p1, k3, [p1, k2] twice.

Row 51 (RS): p1, RT, p2, LT, p2, k1, p7, RT, LT, p2, k1, p2, LT, p3.

Row 52 (WS): [k3, p1] twice, [k2, p1] twice, k7, p1, k2, p1, k4, p1, k1.

Row 53 (RS): p1, LT, p2, RT, p2, k1, p6, RT, p2, LT, p1, k1, p3, LT, p2.

Row 54 (WS): k2, p2, k3, p1, k1, p1, k4, p1, k6, p1, k3, [p1, k2] twice.

Row 55 (RS): p2, LT, RT, p2, RT, p6, LT, p2, RT, p1, k1, p2, RT, LT, p1.

Row 56 (WS): k1, [p1, k2] 4 times, p1, k7, p1, k4, p2, k3.

Row 57 (RS): p3, RT, p2, RT, LT, p6, LT, RT, p2, k1, p1, RT, p2, LT.

Row 58 (WS): p1, k4, p1, k1, p1, k3, p2, k7, p1, k2, p1, k7.

Row 59 (RS): p6, RT, p2, LT, p6, RT, p3, k1, p1, LT, p2, RT.

Row 60 (WS): k1, [p1, k2] twice, p1, k11, p2, k3, p1, k6.

Row 61 (RS): p5, RT, p2, RT, LT, p10, k1, p2, LT, RT, p1.

Row 62 (WS): k2, p2, k3, p1, k10, p1, k2, p1, k3, p1, k5.

Row 63 (RS): p5, k1, p2, RT, p2, LT, p8, RT, p3, LT, p2.

Row 64 (WS): k7, p2, k8, p1, k4, p1, k2, p1, k5.

Row 65 (RS): p5, k1, p2, LT, p2, RT, p7, RT, LT, p6.

Row 66 (WS): k6, p1, k2, p1, k8, p1, k2, p1, k3, p1, k5.

Row 67 (RS): p5, LT, p2, LT, RT, k7, RT, p1, k1, LT, p5.

Row 68 (WS): k5, p1, k2, p1, k1, p1, k8, p2, k3, p2, k5.

Row 69 (RS): p4, RT, LT, p2, LT, p7, RT, [k1, p1] twice, LT, p4.

Row 70 (WS): k4, [p1, k1] twice, p1, k2, p1, k11, p1, k2, p1, k4.

Row 71 (RS): p3, RT, p2, LT, p10, [k1, p1] twice, k1, p2, k1, p4.

Row 72 (WS): k4, [p1, k1] twice, p1, k2, p1, k10, p1, k3, p2, k3.

Row 73 (RS): p2, RT, LT, p2, LT, p9, [k1, p1] twice, k1, p2, k1, p4.

Row 74 (WS): k4, [p1, k1] 3 times, k1, p1, k9, p1, k3, [p1, k2] twice.

Row 75 (RS): p1, RT, p2, LT, p2, k1, p9, LT, [k1, p1] twice, RT, p4.

Row 76 (WS): k5, p1, k2, p1, k1, p1, k10, p1, k2, p1, k4, p1, k1.

Row 77 (RS): p1, LT, p2, RT, p2, k1, p10, LT, p1, k1, RT, p5.

Row 78 (WS): k6, p1, k2, p1, k11, p1, k3, [p1, k2] twice.

Row 79 (RS): p2, LT, RT, p2, RT, p10, RT, p2, LT, p5.

Row 80 (WS): k5, p1, k4, p1, k9, LT, p1, k3, p2, k3.

Row 81 (RS): p3, LT, p2, RT, k1, LT, p7, RT, p4, LT, p4.

Row 82 (WS): k19, p5, k7.

Row 83 (RS): p6, RT, p1, k1, p1, LT, p18.

Row 84 (WS): k18, p2, k1, p1, k1, p2, k6.

Row 85 (RS): p5, RT, [k1, p1] twice, k1, LT p17.

Row 86 (WS): k16, LT, [k1, p1] 3 times, k1, RT, k4.

Row 87 (RS): p3, RT, p2, [k1, p1] 3 times, p1, LT, p15.

Row 88 (WS): k14, LT, k3, [p1, k1] 3 times, k2, RT, k2.

Row 89 (RS): p1, RT, p4, [k1, p1] 3 times, p3, LT, p13.

Row 90 (WS): k13, p1, k4, LT, k1, p1, k1, RT, k4, p1, k1.

Row 91 (RS): RT, p4, k1, p1, RT, p2, k1, p4, LT, p12.

Row 92 (WS): k12, p1, k4, LT, k1, LT, p1, k1, RT, k4, p1.

Row 93 (RS): k1, p3, RT, p1, RT, k1, LT, p1, LT, p3, k1, p12.

Row 94 (WS): k12, p1, k2, LT, k2, [p1, k1] twice, p1, k2, RT, k2, p1.

Row 95 (RS): k1, p1, RT, p2, RT, p1, k1, p1, LT, p2, LT, p1, k1, p12.

Row 96 (WS): k12, p1, LT, k3, [p1, k2] twice, p1, k3, RT, p1.

Row 97 (RS): RT, p3, RT, p2, k1, p2, LT, p3, LT, p12.

Row 98 (WS): k17, [p1, k3] twice, p1, k5.

Row 99 (RS): p4, RT, p3, k1, p3, LT, p16.

Row 100 (WS): k16, [p1, k4] 3 times.

Row 101 (RS): p4, MB, p4, k1, p4, MB, p16.

Row 102 (WS): k21, p1, k9.

Row 103 (RS): p9, MB, p21.

PANEL PAT 2 (WORKED OVER 31 STS)

Row 1 (RS): p5, k1, p17, k1, p7.

Row 2 (WS): k7, p1, k17, p1, k5.

Row 3 (RS): p5, LT, p16, k1, p7.

Row 4 (WS): k7, p1, k16, p1, k6.

Row 5 (RS): p6, LT, p15, k1, p7.

Row 6 (WS): k7, p1, k15, p1, k7.

Row 7 (RS): p7, LT, p14, k1, p7.

Row 8 (WS): k7, p1, k14, p1, k8.

Row 9 (RS): p8, k1, p14, k1, p7.

Row 10 (WS): rep Row 8.

Row 11 (RS): p8, k1, p13, RT, p7.

Row 12 (WS): k7, p2, k13, p1, k8.

Row 13 (RS): p7, RT, p12, RT, LT, p6.

Row 14 (WS): k6, p2, k1, p1, k12, p2, k7.

Row 15 (RS): p6, RT, LT, p10, RT, p1, k1, LT, p5.

Row 16 (WS): k5, p1, k1, p1, k2, p1, k10, p1, k2, p1, k6.

Row 17 (RS): p5, RT, p2, LT, p8, RT, p2, k1, p1, LT, p4.

Row 18 (WS): k4, p1, k2, p1, k3, p1, k8, p2, k3, p1, k5.

Row 19 (RS): p4, RT, p2, RT, LT, p6, RT, p3, k1, p2, LT, p3.

Row 20 (WS): [k3, p1] twice, k3, p2, k6, p1, k2, p1, k3, p1, k4.

Row 21 (RS): p4, k1, p2, RT, p2, LT, p4, RT, LT, p2, k1, p3, LT, p2.

Row 22 (WS): k2, p2, k3, p1, [k2, p1] twice, [k4, p1] twice, k2, p1, k4.

Row 23 (RS): p4, k1, p2, LT, p2, RT, p3, RT, p2, LT, p1, k1, p2, RT, LT, p1.

Row 24 (WS): k1, [p1, k2] twice, p1, k1, [p1, k4] twice, p1, k2, p1, k3, p1, k4.

Row 25 (RS): p4, LT, p2, LT, RT, p4, LT, p2, RT, p1, k1, p1, RT, p2, LT.

Row 26 (WS): p1, k4, p1, k1, [p1, k2] twice, p1, k6, p2, k4, p1, k4.

Row 27 (RS): p3, RT, LT, p2, LT, p6, LT, RT, p2, k1, p1, LT, p2, RT.

Row 28 (WS): k1, [p1, k2] twice, p1, k3, p2, k11, p1, k2, p1, k3.

Row 29 (RS): p2, RT, p2, LT, p10, RT, p3, k1, p2, LT, RT, p1.

Row 30 (WS): k2, p2, k3, p1, k15, p1, k3, p2, k2.

Row 31 (RS): p1, RT, LT, p2, LT, p13, RT, p3, LT, p2.

Row 32 (WS): k7, p2, k13, p1, k3, p1, k2, p1, k1.

Row 33 (RS): RT, p2, LT, p2, k1, p12, RT, LT, p6.

Row 34 (WS): k6, p2, k1, p1, k12, p1, k2, p1, k4, p1.

Row 35 (RS): LT, p2, RT, p2, k1, p11, RT, p1, k1, LT, p5.

Row 36 (WS): k5, p1, k1, p1, k2, p1, k11, p1, k3, p1, k2, p1, k1.

Row 37 (RS): p1, LT, RT, p2, RT, p10, RT, p2, k1, p1, LT, p4.

Row 38 (WS): k4, p1, k2, p1, k3, p1, k10, p2, k3, p2, k2.

Row 39 (RS): p2, LT, p2, RT, LT, p8, RT, p3, k1, p2, LT, p3.

Row 40 (WS): [k3, p1] twice, k3, p2, k8, p1, k2, p1, k6.

Row 41 (RS): p5, RT, p2, LT, p6, RT, LT, p2, k1, p3, LT, p2.

Row 42 (WS): k2, p2, k3, p1, [k2, p1] twice, k6, p2, k3, p1, k5.

Row 43 (RS): p4, RT, p2, RT, LT, p4, RT, p2, LT, p1, k1, p2, RT, LT, p1.

Row 44 (WS): k1, p1, [k2, p1] twice, k1, p1, [k4, p1] twice, k2, p1, k3, p1, k4.

Row 45 (RS): p4, k1, p2, RT, p2, LT, p3, LT, p2, RT, p1, k1, p1, RT, p2, LT.

Row 46 (WS): p1, k4, p1, k1, [p1, k2] twice, [p1, k4] twice, p1, k2, p1, k4.

Row 47 (RS): p4, k1, p2, LT, p2, RT, p4, LT, RT, p2, k1, p1, LT, p2, RT.

Row 48 (WS): k1, [p1, k2] twice, p1, k3, p2, k6, p1, k2, p1, k3, p1, k4.

Row 49 (RS): p4, LT, p2, LT, RT, p6, [RT, p2] twice, LT, RT, p1.

Row 50 (WS): k2, p2, k3, p2, k11, p2, k4, p1, k4.

Row 51 (RS): p3, RT, LT, p2, LT, p10, RT, k1, p3, LT, p2.

Row 52 (WS): k7, p1, k1, p1, k14, p1, k2, p1, k3.

Row 53 (RS): p2, RT, p2, LT, p12, RT, p1, LT, p6.

Row 54 (WS): k6, p2, k2, p1, k12, p1, k3, p2, k2.

Row 55 (RS): p1, RT, LT, p2, LT, p10, RT, p2, k1, LT, p5.

Row 56 (WS): k5, p1, k1, p1, k3, p1, k10, p1, k3, p1, k2, p1, k1.

Row 57 (RS): RT, p2, LT, p2, k1, p9, RT, p3, k1, p1, LT, p4.

Row 58 (WS): k4, p1, k2, p1, k3, p2, k9, p1, k2, p1, k4, p1.

Row 59 (RS): LT, p2, RT, p2, k1, p8, RT, LT, p2, k1, p2, LT, p3.

Row 60 (WS): [k3, p1] twice, [k2, p1] twice, k8, p1, k3, p1, k2, p1, k1.

Row 61 (RS): p1, LT, RT, p3, k1, p7, RT, p2, LT, p1, k1, p3, LT, p2.

Row 62 (WS): k2, p2, k3, p1, k1, p1, k4, p1, k7, p1, k4, p2, k2.

Row 63 (RS): p2, LT, p3, RT, p7, LT, p2, RT, p1, k1, p2, RT, LT, p1.

Row 64 (WS): k1, [p1, k2] 4 times, p1, k7, LT, p1, k7.

Row 65 (RS): p6, RT, k1, LT, p6, LT, RT, p2, k1, p1, RT, p2, LT.

Row 66 (WS): p1, k4, p1, k1, p1, k3, p2, k6, LT, p3, RT, k5.

Row 67 (RS): p4, RT, [k1, p1] twice, k1, LT, p5, RT, p3, k1, p1, LT, p2, RT.

Row 68 (WS): k1, p1, [k2, p1] twice, k9, LT, [k1, p1] 3 times, k1, RT, p3.

Row 69 (RS): p2, RT, p2, [k1, p1] twice, k1, p2, LT, p8, k1, p2, LT, RT, p1.

Row 70 (WS): k2, p2, k3, p1, k7, LT,

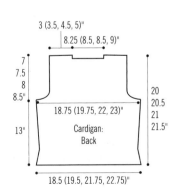

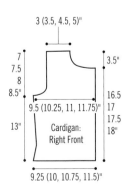

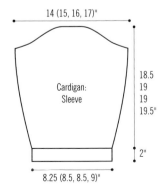

k3, [p1, k1] 3 times, k2, RT, k1.

Row 71 (RS): RT, p3, RT, [p1, k1] twice, p4, k1, p7, k1, p3, LT, p2.

Row 72 (WS): [k7, p1] twice, k3, LT, k1, p1, k7, p1.

Row 73 (RS): k1, p3, RT, p1, RT, p2, k1, p3, k1, p6, RT, p7.

Row 74 (WS): k7, p2, k6, p1, k2, LT, k2, p2, k2, RT, k2, p1.

Row 75 (RS): k1, p1, RT, p2, RT, LT, p2, LT, p1, k1, p5, RT, LT, p6.

Row 76 (WS): k6, p2, k1, p1, k5, p1, LT, p1, [k2, p1] 3 times, RT, p1.

Row 77 (RS): RT, p1, k1, p1, RT, p2, LT, p1, k1, p1, LT, p4, RT, p1, k1, LT, p5.

Row 78 (WS): k5, p1, k1, p1, k2, p1, k7, p1, k1, p1, k4, p1, k1, p1, k3.

Row 79 (RS): p3, k1, p1, LT, p2, RT, p1, k1, p6, RT, p1, RT, p1, LT, p4.

Row 80 (WS): k4, p1, k2, p2, k2, p1, k6, p1, [k2, p1] 3 times, k3.

Row 81 (RS): p3, MB, p2, LT, RT, p2, MB, p5, RT, p1, RT, LT, p1, LT, p3.

Row 82 (WS): k3, [p1, k2] 3 times, p1, k9, p2, k7.

Row 83 (RS): p7, LT, p8, RT, p1, RT, p2, LT, p1, LT, p2.

Row 84 (WS): [k2, p1] twice, k4, p1, k2, p1, k17.

Row 85 (RS): p17, LT, p1, LT, p2, RT, p1, RT, p2.

Row 86 (WS): k3, [p1, k2] 3 times, p1, k18.

Row 87 (RS): p18, LT, p1, LT, RT, p1, RT, p3.

Row 88 (WS): k4, p1, k2, p2, k2, p1, k19.

Row 89 (RS): p18, RT, p2, RT, p2, LT, p3.

Row 90 (WS): k3, p1, k8, p1, k18.

Row 91 (RS): p17, RT, p1, MB, p3, MB, p2, LT, p2.

Row 92 (WS): knit.

Row 93 (RS): p22, MB, p8.

CARDIGAN RIGHT FRONT

Cast on 51 (55, 59, 63) sts.

Work seed st band for 20 rows as follows:

Row 1 (RS): p1, *k1, p1*, rep from * to end of row.

Following rows: k the p sts and p the k sts; AT THE SAME TIME, shape side seam as follows: dec 1 st at side seam on 9th row, then on 15th row, to 49 (53, 57, 61) sts.

Begin working main pat, placing pat as follows:

Row 1 (RS): work 9 sts for band in seed st pat as established, p4, work Row 1 of Chart I, reading row from right to left (or work Row 1 of Panel Pat 1), p to last 2 sts, p2tog.

Row 2 (WS): k4 (8, 12, 16), work Row 2 of Chart I, reading row from left to right (or work Row 2 of Panel Pat 1), k4, work 9 sts seed st. Pat is now in position.

Continue working chart or panel pat as established, and work 1 more dec at side seam on Row 7 of chart. You should now have 47 (51, 55, 59) sts. Work even (no decs) in pat until piece measures 3½" from bottom edge, then inc 1 st at side seam on next RS row, then every following 10th row until you have 52 (56, 60, 64) sts.

Work even in pat, if necessary, until piece measures 13" from bottom edge, ending with WS facing for next row.

Armhole shaping: bind off sts at the beginning of WS rows in the following sequence: bind off 3 sts twice, bind off 2 sts twice, bind off 1 st twice. You should now have 40 (44, 48, 52) sts.

Work even until chart (or panel pat) is complete, then continue in reverse st st with seed st band until piece measures 3½ (4, 4½, 5)" from beginning of armhole shaping, ending with RS facing for next row.

Neck shaping: work seed st pat across first 9 sts, then slip these sts to stitch holder. Continuing in reverse st st, bind off sts at beginning of RS rows in the following sequence: bind off 4 sts twice, bind off 2 sts twice, bind off 1 st 2 (4, 2, 4) times. You should now have 17 (19, 25, 27) sts remaining for shoulder. Work even in pat until piece measures 7 (7½, 8, 8½)" from beginning of armhole shaping, ending with RS facing for next row. Bind off all sts.

CARDIGAN LEFT FRONT

Cast on 51 (55, 59, 63) sts and work seed st band as for Right Front, to 49 (53, 57, 61) sts.

Begin working main pat, placing pat as follows:

Row 1 (RS): p2tog, p3 (7, 11, 15); work Row 1 of Chart II, reading row from right to left (or work Row 1 of Panel Pat 2); p4; work 9 sts for band in seed st pat as established.

Row 2 (WS): work 9 sts seed st; k4; work Row 2 of Chart II, reading row from left to right (or work Row 2 of Panel Pat 2); k to end of row. Pat is now in position.

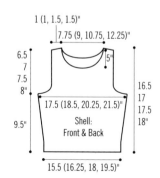

1 (1, 1.5, 1.5)"
7.75 (9, 10.75, 12.25)"
6.5
7
7.5
8"
5"
16.5
17
17.5
18"
9.5"
17.5 (18.5, 20.25, 21.5)"
Shell:
Front & Back
15.5 (16.25, 18, 19.5)"

Chart I

□ k on RS, p on WS

− p on RS, k on WS

● MB: Make Bobble (see Special Abbreviations)

RT: Right Twist (see Special Abbreviations)

LT: Left Twist (see Special Abbreviations)

QUICK TIP: *If you're prone to wrist or hand strain, try switching to bamboo or wood needles; they're lighter in weight and, in the long run, easier on the hands.*

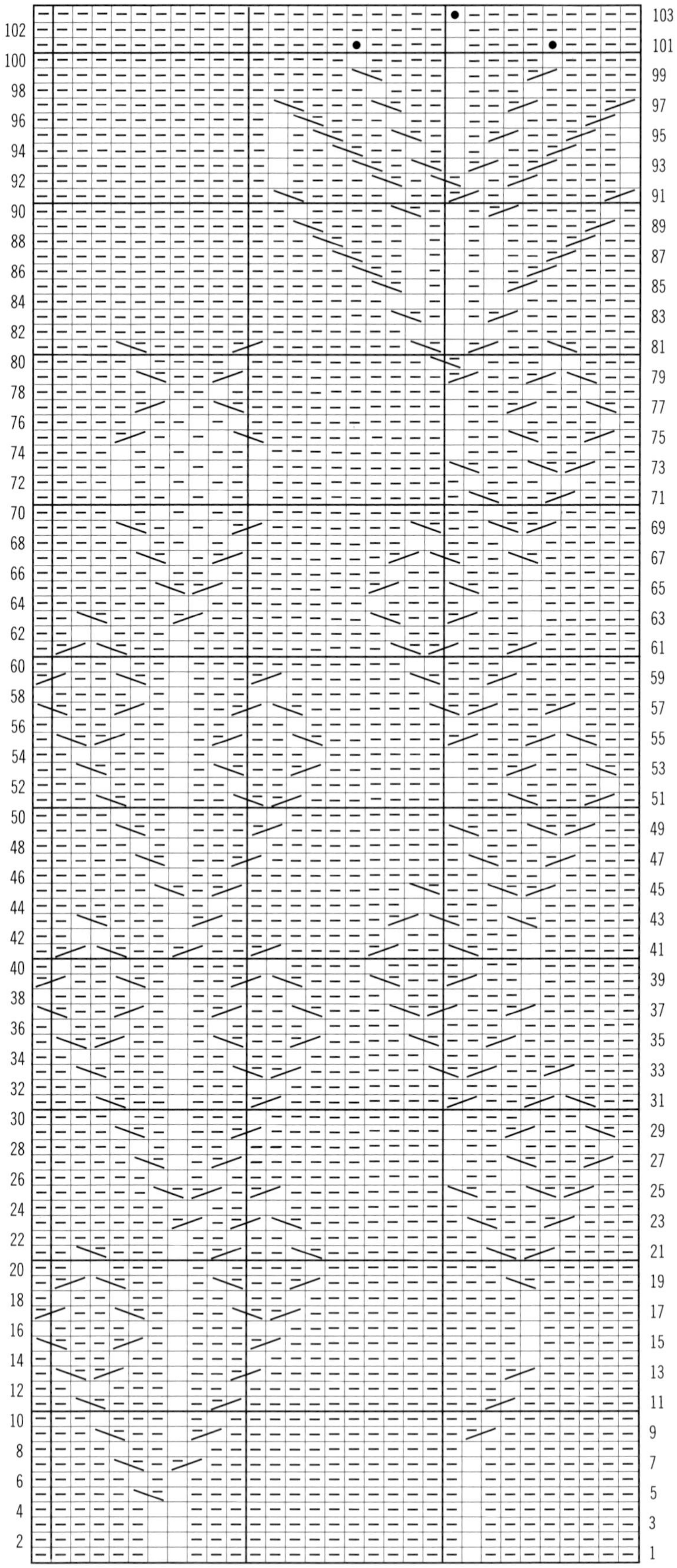

Chart = 31 sts wide

Chart II

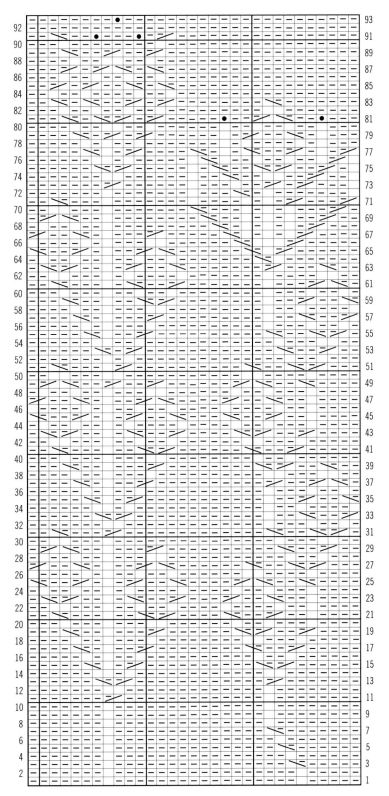

Chart = 31 sts wide

Continue working chart or panel pat as established, and work 1 more dec at side seam on Row 7 of chart. You should now have 47 (51, 55, 59) sts. Work even (no decs) in pat until piece measures 3½" from bottom edge, then inc 1 st at side seam on next RS row, then every following 10th row until you have 52 (56, 60, 64) sts.

Work even in pat, if necessary, until piece measures 13" from bottom edge, ending with RS facing for next row.

Armhole shaping: bind off sts at the beginning of RS rows in the following sequence: bind off 3 sts twice, bind off 2 sts twice, bind off 1 st twice. You should now have 40 (44, 48, 52) sts.

Work even until chart or panel pat is complete, then continue in reverse st st with seed st band until piece measures 3½ (4, 4½, 5)" from beginning of armhole shaping, ending with WS facing for next row.

Neck shaping: work seed st pat across first 9 sts, then slip these sts to stitch holder. Continuing in reverse st st, bind off sts at beginning of WS rows in the following sequence: bind off 4 sts twice, bind off 2 sts twice, bind off 1 st 2 (4, 2, 4) times. You should now have 17 (19, 25, 27) sts remaining for shoulder. Work even in pat until piece measures 7 (7½, 8, 8½)" from beginning of armhole shaping, ending with RS facing for next row. Bind off all sts.

CARDIGAN BACK

Cast on 101 (107, 119, 125) sts and work 20 rows seed st band; AT THE SAME TIME, shape side seam as follows: dec 1 st at each side on 9th row, then on 15th row, to 97 (103, 115, 121) sts.

Begin working Charts I and II (or Panel Pats 1 and 2), placing pats as follows:

Row 1 (RS): p2tog; p13 (16, 22, 25); work Row 1 of Chart II, reading row from right to left (or work Row 1 of Panel Pat 2); p5; work Row 1 of Chart I, reading row from right to left (or work Row 1 of Panel Pat 1); p to last 2 sts; p2tog.

Row 2 (WS): k14 (17, 23, 26); work Row 2 of Chart I, reading row from left to right (or work Row 2 of Panel Pat 1); k5; work Row 2 of Chart II (or work Row 2 of Panel Pat 2), reading row from left to right; k to end of row. Charted pats are now in position.

Continue working chart or panel pat as established, and work 1 more dec at side seam on Row 7 of chart. You should now have 93 (99, 111, 117) sts. Work even (no decs) in pat until piece measures 3½" from bottom edge, then inc 1 st at each side on next RS row, then every following 10th row until you have 103 (109, 121, 127) sts.

Work even in pat, if necessary, until piece measures 13" from bottom edge, ending with RS facing for next row.

Armhole shaping: bind off sts at the beginning of each row in the following sequence: bind off 3 sts at each side twice, bind off 2 sts at each side twice, bind off 1 st at each side twice. You should now have 79 (85, 97, 103) sts.

Work even until charts are complete, then continue in reverse st st until piece measures 6 (6½, 7, 7½)" from beginning of armhole shaping, ending with RS facing for next row.

Neck shaping: p17 (19, 25, 27). Join 2nd ball of yarn to next st and with 2nd ball, bind off 45 (47, 47, 49) sts for

back neck, then p to end. Work even on both sides with separate balls in reverse st st until piece measures 7 (7½, 8, 8½)" from beginning of armhole shaping, ending with RS facing for next row. Bind off all sts.

CARDIGAN SLEEVE

Cast on 45 (47, 47, 49) sts.

Work 20 rows seed st, ending with RS facing for next row.

Proceed in reverse st st; AT THE SAME TIME, inc 1 at each side every 6th (6th, 4th, 4th) row 13 (16, 9, 13) times, then every 8th (8th, 6th, 6th) row 3 (1, 11, 9) time(s), to 77 (81, 87, 93) sts. Work even until piece measures 17 (17½, 17½, 18)" from bottom edge, ending with RS facing for next row.

Sleeve cap shaping: continuing in pat, bind off sts at the beginning of each row in the following sequence: bind off 4 sts 3 (2, 4, 4) time(s), bind off 3 sts 2 (3, 2, 2) times, bind off 2 sts 2 (3, 2, 3) times, bind off 1 st 2 (1, 1, 1) time(s), bind off 2 sts 1 (2, 1, 1) time(s), bind off 3 sts once.

Next Row (RS): bind off remaining 19 (19, 23, 25) sts.

SHELL FRONT

Cast on 85 (89, 99, 107) sts.

Work seed st band as follows:

Row 1 (RS): p1, *k1, p1*, rep from * to end of row.

Following rows: k the p sts and p the k sts.

Rep the last row until piece measures 2" from bottom edge, ending with RS facing for next row.

Proceed in reverse st st as given for Gauge Swatch; AT THE SAME TIME, shape sides as follows: inc 1 st at side on 1st row, then every 8th row 5 times, to 97 (101, 111, 119) sts.

Work even in pat, if necessary, until piece measures 9½" from bottom edge, ending with RS facing for next row.

Armhole shaping: bind off sts at the beginning of each row in the following sequence: bind off 4 sts at each side 4 (4, 3, 3) times; bind off 2 sts at each side twice, bind off 1 st at each side 1 (0, 2, 2) time(s). You should now have 55 (61, 75, 83) sts.

Work even until piece measures 2 (2½, 3, 3½)" from beginning of armhole shaping, ending with RS facing for next row.

Left neck shaping: p21 (23, 28, 30). Leave remaining sts on a stitch holder. Continuing in reverse st st, bind off sts at beginning of WS rows in the following sequence: bind off 4 sts twice, bind off 2 sts 2 (2, 3, 3) times, bind off 1 st 3 (5, 6, 8) times. You should now have 6 (6, 8, 8) sts remaining for shoulder. Work even in pat until piece measures 6½ (7, 7½, 8)" from beginning of armhole shaping, ending with RS facing for next row.

Next row (RS): bind off 3 (3, 4, 4) sts, p to end of row.

Next row (WS): knit.

Next row (RS): bind off remaining 3 (3, 4, 4) sts.

Right neck shaping: with RS facing, bind off 13 (15, 19, 23) sts. Continuing in reverse st st, bind off sts at beginning of RS rows in the following sequence: bind off 4 sts twice, bind off 2 sts 2 (2, 3, 3) times, bind off 1 st 3 (5, 6, 8) times. You should now have 6 (6, 8, 8) sts remaining for shoulder. Work even in pat until piece measures 6½ (7, 7½, 8)" from beginning of armhole shaping, ending with WS facing for next row.

Next row (WS): bind off 3 (3, 4, 4) sts, k to end of row.

Next row (RS): purl.

Next row (WS): bind off remaining 3 (3, 4, 4) sts.

SHELL BACK

Work as given for Front up to and including armhole shaping.

Work even until piece measures 4 (4½, 5, 5½)" from beginning of armhole shaping, ending with RS facing for next row.

Right neck shaping: p16 (17, 21, 23). Leave remaining sts on a stitch holder. Continuing in reverse st st, bind off sts at beginning of WS rows in the following sequence: bind off 2 sts 3 times, bind off 1 st 4 (5, 7, 9) times. You should now have 6 (6, 8, 8) sts remaining for shoulder. Work even in pat until piece measures 6½ (7, 7½, 8)" from beginning of armhole shaping, ending with RS facing for next row.

Next row (RS): bind off 3 (3, 4, 4) sts, p to end of row.

Next row (WS): knit.

Next row (RS): bind off remaining 3 (3, 4, 4) sts.

Left neck shaping: with RS facing, bind off 23 (27, 33, 37) sts. Continuing in reverse st st, bind off sts at beginning of RS rows in the following sequence: bind off 2 sts 3 times, bind off 1 st 4 (5, 7, 9) times. You should now have 6 (6, 8, 8) sts remaining for shoulder. Work even in pat until piece measures 6½ (7, 7½, 8)" from beginning of armhole shaping, ending with WS facing for next row.

Next row (WS): bind off 3 (3, 4, 4) sts, k to end of row.

Next row (RS): purl.

Next row (WS): bind off remaining 3 (3, 4, 4) sts.

FINISHING

CARDIGAN

Pin pieces to measurements as shown and block as directed for Gauge Swatch. Sew shoulder seams.

Neckband: with RS facing, work seed st pat across Right Front stitch holder; pick up and knit 23 (23, 25, 25) sts along Right Front neck edge, pick up and knit 2 sts down right side of Back neck edge, pick up and knit 45 (47, 47, 49) sts along horizontal Back neck edge, pick up and knit 2 sts up left side of Back neck edge, pick up and knit 23 (23, 25, 25) sts along Left Front neck edge, work seed st pat across Left Front stitch holder. You should have a total of 113 (115, 119, 121) sts. Keeping continuity of seed st pat, work seed st for

collar until collar measures 1½" deep from beginning, ending with RS facing for next row. Bind off in pat.

Button loops: use pins to mark 7 evenly spaced button loops along Right Front edge, placing first pin at hem edge and last pin at upper edge of collar. With RS facing you, tie on yarn to Right Front opening at hem edge. Work single crochet on first edge st of Front opening (see page 124). *Form single chain button loop as follows: [wrap yarn around hook (without inserting hook through Front edge), then pull through loop on hook], rep from [to] twice more, resume single crochet along edge to next pin marker.* Rep from * to * to last marker, then make 1 more button loop. Finish at top with 1 st single crochet. Cut yarn and pull through last loop on hook to finish.

Sew side seams and sleeve seams. Matching center of sleeve cap to shoulder seam, sew in sleeves. Sew buttons to correspond to button loops.

SHELL

Pin pieces to measurements as shown and block as directed for Gauge Swatch. Sew right shoulder.

Neckband: with RS facing, pick up and knit 34 (36, 40, 44) sts along Left Front neck edge, pick up and knit 34 (36, 40, 44) sts along Left Front neck edge, pick up and knit 57 (61, 69, 77) sts along Back neck edge. You should have a total of 125 (133, 149, 165) sts. Work 5 rows seed st. Bind off in pat.

Sew left shoulder and neckband seam.

Arm trims: with RS facing, pick up and knit 83 (89, 95, 101) sts along armhole edge. Work 5 rows seed st. Bind off in pat.

Sew arm trim and side seams. 🍃

jilly twinset

A simple, spare cardigan and funnel-neck top with cap sleeves are the perfect shapes
to highlight the texture and beauty of this ribbon yarn. Against a backdrop of easy garter stitch,
the yarn's pearlescent sheen and delicate pink color evoke the lining of a seashell.

SKILL LEVEL: VERY EASY

MEASUREMENTS

SIZES (in inches)	TEENS			WOMEN			
	12	14	16	SM	MD	LG	XL
Cardigan Finished Chest	30½	33½	35	37	40	42½	45½
Cardigan Finished Length	16	17	18	19	20	21	22
Pullover Finished Chest	29	31	34½	36	38½	41	44
Pullover Finished Length	14	15	16	17	18	19	20

MATERIALS

Yarn: Berocco Glacé 100% Rayon (75 yds or 69 m/50 gr skein).
See also page 126 for yarn information.

NO. OF SKEINS	TEENS			WOMEN			
	12	14	16	SM	MD	LG	XL
Cardigan, #2439	9	10	12	13	15	17	18
Pullover, #2439	7	7	9	10	11	12	14

Needles: 1 pr. U.S. size 7 (4.5 mm) needles OR SIZE TO
OBTAIN GAUGE

U.S. size 7 (4.5 mm) crochet hook for cardigan

Spare needle or stitch holder

Three ³/₄" buttons for cardigan

GAUGE

20 sts and 36 rows = 4" in garter st

To work Gauge Swatch: cast on 22 sts and work garter st (k all
sts on all rows) until piece measures 4" from bottom edge. Bind
off. Block swatch by laying flat and applying lots of steam with
steam iron held just above the swatch. Let cool and dry. If you
have too many sts and rows to the inch, change to a larger
needle; too few means you should use a smaller needle.

*Your garment will not fit properly if the tension gauge is
incorrect! Take the time to check by making gauge swatch.*

*Directions are given for Teens' size 12. Teens' sizes 14, 16,
and Women's sizes Small, Medium, Large, and Extra-Large
are given in parentheses. Where there is only one number, it
applies to all sizes.*

CARDIGAN BACK

Cast on 70 (78, 82, 86, 94, 100, 108) sts. Work 6 rows
garter stitch. *Next row (RS): k1, sl 1, k1, psso, k to last 3 sts,
k2tog, k1. Work 5 rows garter st.* Rep from * to * twice more.
You should now have 64 (72, 76, 80, 88, 94, 102) sts. Work
even, if necessary, until piece measures 3" from bottom edge,
ending with RS facing for next row.

Work 6 rows garter stitch. *Next row (RS): k1, inc 1, k to last
2 sts, inc 1, k1. Work 7 (7, 7, 7, 9, 9, 11) rows garter st.*
Rep from * to * 5 more times, until you have 76 (84, 88, 92,
100, 106, 114) sts.

Work even, if necessary, until piece measures 9 (9½, 10, 10½,
11, 11½, 12)" from bottom edge, ending with RS facing for
next row.

Raglan shaping (RS): k3, sl 1, k1, psso, k to last 5 sts,
k2tog, k3.

Next row (WS): k2, p1, k to last 3 sts, p1, k2. Rep the last 2
rows 22 (24, 25, 27, 30, 33, 36) more times, until you have
30 (34, 36, 36, 38, 38, 40) sts remaining.

Work even, if necessary, until piece measures 5½ (6, 6½, 7,
7½, 8, 8½)" from beginning of raglan shaping, ending with RS
facing for next row. Bind off.

CARDIGAN RIGHT FRONT

Cast on 35 (39, 41, 43, 47, 50, 53) sts. Work 6 rows garter
stitch. *Next row (RS): k to last 3 sts, k2tog, k1. Work 5 rows
garter st.* Rep from * to * twice more. You should now have
32 (36, 38, 40, 44, 47, 50) sts. Work even, if necessary, until
piece measures 3" from bottom edge, ending with RS facing for
next row.

Work 6 rows garter stitch. *Next row (RS): k to last 2 sts, inc 1, k1. Work 7 (7, 7, 7, 9, 9, 11) rows garter st.* Rep from * to * 5 more times until you have 38 (42, 44, 46, 50, 53, 56) sts.

Work even, if necessary, until piece measures 9 (9½, 10, 10½, 11, 11½, 12)" from bottom edge, ending with RS facing for next row.

Raglan and neck shaping:

Sizes 12, 14, 16, SM, MD only:
Next row (RS): k1, sl 1, k1, psso, k to last 5 sts, k2tog, k3.

Next row (WS): k2, p1, k to end. Rep the last 2 rows 2 (4, 5, 3, 2) more times.

All sizes
Next row (RS): k to last 5 sts, k2tog, k3.

Next row (WS): k2, p1, k to end.

Next row (RS): k1, sl 1, k1, psso, k to last 5 sts, k2tog, k3.

Next row (WS): k2, p1, k to end. Rep the last 4 rows 9 (9, 9, 11, 13, 16, 17) more times. Upon completion of raglan shaping and neck shaping, you should have 2 sts remaining. Break yarn and draw through remaining sts to fasten.

CARDIGAN LEFT FRONT

Cast on 35 (39, 41, 43, 47, 50, 53) sts. Work 6 rows garter stitch. *Next row (RS): k1, k2tog, k to end of row.

Work 5 rows garter st.* Rep from * to * twice more. You should now have 32 (36, 38, 40, 44, 47, 50) sts. Work even, if necessary, until piece measures 3" from bottom edge, ending with RS facing for next row.

Work 6 rows garter stitch. *Next row (RS): k1, inc 1, k to end of row. Work 7 (7, 7, 7, 9, 9, 11) rows garter st.* Rep from * to * 5 more times until you have 38 (42, 44, 46, 50, 53, 56) sts.

Work even, if necessary, until piece measures 9 (9½, 10, 10½, 11, 11½, 12)" from bottom edge, ending with RS facing for next row.

Raglan and neck shaping:

Sizes 12, 14, 16, SM, MD only
Next row (RS): k3, sl 1, k1, psso, k to last 3 sts, k2tog, k1.

Next row (WS): k to last 3 sts, p1, k2. Rep the last 2 rows 2 (4, 5, 3, 2) more times.

All sizes
Next row (RS): k3, sl 1, k1, psso, k to end.

Next row (WS): k to last 3 sts, p1, k2.

Next row (RS): k3, sl 1, k1, psso, k to last 3 sts, k2tog, k1.

Next row (WS): k to last 3 sts, p1, k2. Rep the last 4 rows 9 (9, 9, 11, 13, 16, 17) more times. Upon completion of raglan shaping and neck shaping, you should have 2 sts remaining. Break yarn and draw through remaining sts to fasten.

Cast on 30 (32, 36, 38, 40, 42, 46) sts.

Proceed in garter st and inc 1 at each side on 5th row, and every following 6th row 1 (1, 3, 5, 8, 9, 10) times, then every 8th row 11 (12, 11, 10, 9, 9, 9) times until you have 56 (60, 66, 70, 76, 80, 86) sts.

Work even, if necessary, until piece measures 14 (14½, 15, 15½, 16, 16½, 17)" from bottom edge, ending with RS facing for next row.

Raglan shaping:

Next row (RS): k3, sl 1, k1, psso, k to last 5 sts, k2tog, k3.

Next row (WS): k2, p1, k to last 3 sts, p1, k2.

Rep the last 2 rows 18 (20, 23, 25, 28, 30, 34) more times.

Next row (RS): k3, sl 1, k1, psso, k to last 5 sts, k2tog, k3.

Next row (WS): k2, p1, k to last 3 sts, p1, k2.

Next row (RS): knit.

Next row (WS): k2, p1, k to last 3 sts, p1, k2.

Rep the last 4 rows 1 (1, 1, 1, 1, 0) more time, until you have 14 sts remaining.

Work even, if necessary, until length of raglan seam matches length of Back raglan seam, ending with RS facing for next row. Bind off.

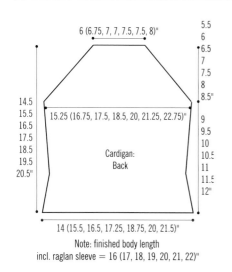

6 (6.75, 7, 7, 7.5, 7.5, 8)"

5.5
6
6.5
7
7.5
8
8.5"

14.5
15.5
16.5
17.5
18.5
19.5
20.5"

15.25 (16.75, 17.5, 18.5, 20, 21.25, 22.75)"

9
9.5
10
10.5
11
11.5
12"

Cardigan:
Back

14 (15.5, 16.5, 17.25, 18.75, 20, 21.5)"
Note: finished body length
incl. raglan sleeve = 16 (17, 18, 19, 20, 21, 22)"

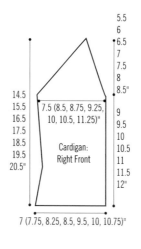

5.5
6
6.5
7
7.5
8
8.5"

14.5
15.5
16.5
17.5
18.5
19.5
20.5"

7.5 (8.5, 8.75, 9.25, 10, 10.5, 11.25)"

9
9.5
10
10.5
11
11.5
12"

Cardigan:
Right Front

7 (7.75, 8.25, 8.5, 9.5, 10, 10.75)"

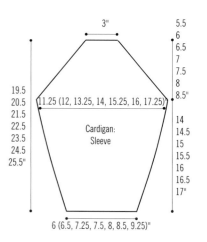

3"

5.5
6
6.5
7
7.5
8
8.5"

19.5
20.5
21.5
22.5
23.5
24.5
25.5"

11.25 (12, 13.25, 14, 15.25, 16, 17.25)"

14
14.5
15
15.5
16
16.5
17"

Cardigan:
Sleeve

6 (6.5, 7.25, 7.5, 8, 8.5, 9.25)"

PULLOVER FRONT

Cast on 56 (62, 70, 74, 80, 86, 94) sts.

Work 8 rows garter stitch. *Next row (RS): k1, inc 1, k to last 2 sts, inc 1, k1. Work 5 (7, 7, 7, 9, 9, 9) rows garter st.* Rep from * to * 7 more times until you have 72 (78, 86, 90, 96, 102, 110) sts.

Work even, if necessary, until piece measures 8 (8½, 9, 9½, 10, 10½, 11)" from bottom edge, ending with RS facing for next row.

Raglan shaping (RS): Bind off 2 sts at beginning of next 2 rows.

Next row (RS): k3, sl 1, k1, psso, k to last 5 sts, k2tog, k3.

Next row (WS): k2, p1, k to last 3 sts, p1, k2. Rep the last 2 rows 19 (21, 24, 26, 27, 30, 33) more times, until you have 28 (30, 32, 32, 36, 36, 38) sts remaining.

Work even, if necessary, until piece measures 5 (5½, 6, 6½, 7, 7½, 8)" from beginning of raglan shaping, ending with RS facing for next row. Leave remaining sts on spare needle or holder.

PULLOVER BACK

Work exactly as for Front.

PULLOVER SLEEVES

Cast on 40 (44, 50, 54, 60, 64, 70) sts. Work 4 rows garter stitch.

Next row (RS): k1, inc 1, k to last 2 sts, inc 1, k1. Work 3 rows garter st. Rep from * to * twice more, until you have 46 (50, 56, 60, 66, 70, 76) sts.

Work even, if necessary, until piece measures 2" from bottom edge, ending with RS facing for next row.

Raglan shaping (RS): Bind off 2 sts at beginning of next 2 rows.

Next row (RS): k3, sl 1, k1, psso, k to last 5 sts, k2tog, k3.

Next row (WS): k2, p1, k to last 3 sts, p1, k2. Rep the last 2 rows 12 (14, 17, 19, 22, 24, 27) more times.

Next row (RS): k3, sl 1, k1, psso, k to last 5 sts, k2tog, k3.

Next row (WS): k2, p1, k to last 3 sts, p1, k2.

Next row (RS): knit.

Next row (WS): k2, p1, k to last 3 sts, p1, k2. Rep the last 4 rows twice more until you have 10 sts remaining.

Work even, if necessary, until length of raglan seam matches length of Back raglan seam, ending with RS facing for next row. Leave remaining sts on spare needle or holder.

FINISHING

CARDIGAN

Sew raglan seams. Sew side seams and sleeve seams.

Front edging: with RS facing you, tie on yarn to Right Front opening at hem edge. Work single crochet along Front opening (see Knitting and Finishing Techniques on page 124).

Note: As you crochet along edge, make sure that you're picking up enough loops of edge so that the crochet is not pulling up the Front.

Continue single crochet until you are 4" below beginning of Right Front V-neck shaping. *Form single chain button loop as follows: [wrap yarn around hook (without inserting hook through Front edge), then pull through loop on hook], rep from [to] until chain is 1" long, resume single crochet along edge for another 1½"*. Rep from * to * once more, then make 1 more button loop.

Continue single crochet along Right Front V-neck, top of right sleeve, Back neck edge, top of left sleeve, and Left Front edge to hem. Cut yarn and pull through last loop on hook to finish.

Sew buttons on Left Front to correspond to button loops on Right Front.

PULLOVER

Sew raglan seams, leaving left Back raglan seam open.

Collar: with RS facing, knit across 28 (30, 32, 32, 36, 36, 38) sts from Back stitch holder, knit across 10 sts from right sleeve stitch holder, knit across 28 (30, 32, 32, 36, 36, 38) sts from Front stitch holder, and knit across 10 sts from left sleeve stitch holder. You should have a total of 76 (80, 84, 84, 92, 92, 96) sts. Work collar in garter st until length from beginning of collar measures 3", ending with RS facing for next row. Bind off.

Sew left Back raglan seam and collar seam. Sew side and sleeve seams.

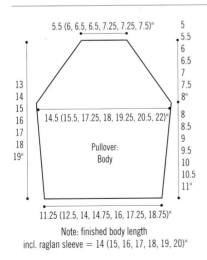

5.5 (6, 6.5, 6.5, 7.25, 7.25, 7.5)"

5
5.5
6
6.5
7
7.5
8"
8
8.5
9
9.5
10
10.5
11"

13
14
15
16
17
18
19"

14.5 (15.5, 17.25, 18, 19.25, 20.5, 22)"

Pullover: Body

11.25 (12.5, 14, 14.75, 16, 17.25, 18.75)"
Note: finished body length
incl. raglan sleeve = 14 (15, 16, 17, 18, 19, 20)"

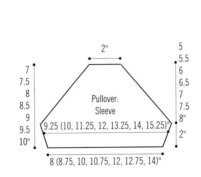

2"

5
5.5
6
6.5
7
7.5
8"
2"

7
7.5
8
8.5
9
9.5
10"

Pullover: Sleeve

9.25 (10, 11.25, 12, 13.25, 14, 15.25)"

8 (8.75, 10, 10.75, 12, 12.75, 14)"

mariner

A simple tunic with bell sleeves and kangaroo pocket is easy to make in seed stitch and plain knitting. The clean lines of the design are highlighted in a fresh apple green cotton.

SKILL LEVEL: VERY EASY

MEASUREMENTS

SIZES (in inches)	TEENS			WOMEN			
	12	14	16	SM	MD	LG	XL
Finished Chest	35	37	39	42	44	47	49
Finished Length	26	27	28	29	29½	30	30½

MATERIALS

Yarn: Schoeller Esslinger Palma 100% Mercerized Cotton DK (119 yds or 110 m/50 gr ball). *See also page 126 for yarn information.*

NO. OF BALLS	TEENS			WOMEN			
	12	14	16	SM	MD	LG	XL
#15 Apple Green	9	10	11	12	13	14	15

Needles: 1 pr. U.S. size 6 (4 mm) needles OR SIZE TO OBTAIN GAUGE

U.S. size 6 (4 mm) circular needle, 24" or 29" (60 cm or 75 cm) long

Spare needle or stitch holder

GAUGE

22 sts and 26 rows = 4" in st st

To work Gauge Swatch: cast on 24 sts and work st st (k all sts on RS and p all sts on WS) until piece measures 4" from bottom edge. Bind off. Block swatch by laying flat and applying lots of steam with steam iron held just above the swatch. Let cool and dry. If you have too many sts and rows to the inch, change to a larger needle; too few means you should use a smaller needle.

Your garment will not fit properly if the tension gauge is incorrect! Take the time to check by making gauge swatch.

Directions are given for Teens' size 12. Teens' sizes 14, 16, and Women's sizes Small, Medium, Large, and Extra-Large are given in parentheses. Where there is only one number, it applies to all sizes.

FRONT

Note: three hem sections are worked separately, then joined at top of slits.

Right Front hem: cast on 26 (28, 30, 34, 36, 40, 42) sts.

Work seed st band as follows:

Row 1 (RS): *p1, k1*, rep from * to end of row.

Following rows: k the p sts and p the k sts.

Work 8 more rows in seed st, ending with RS facing for next row.

Next row (RS): work 7 sts seed st in pat as established, k to end of row.

Next row (WS): p19 (21, 23, 27, 29, 33, 35), work 7 sts seed st.

Rep the last 2 rows until piece measures 3" from bottom edge, ending with RS facing for next row. Break yarn.

Center Front hem: with Right Front sts on left-hand needle, cast on 45 (45, 47, 47, 49, 49, 51) sts to end of needle.

Work seed st band as follows:

Row 1 (RS): k1, *p1, k1*, rep from * to end of row.

Following rows: k the p sts and p the k sts.

Work 8 more rows in seed st, ending with RS facing for next row.

Next row (RS): work 7 sts seed st in pat as established, k31 (31, 33, 33, 35, 35, 37), work 7 sts seed st in pat as established.

Next row (WS): work 7 sts seed st, p31 (31, 33, 33, 35, 35, 37), work 7 sts seed st.

Rep the last 2 rows until piece measures 3" from bottom edge, ending with RS facing for next row. Break yarn.

Left Front hem: with Right Front and Center Front sts on left-hand needle, cast on 26 (28, 30, 34, 36, 40, 42) sts to end of needle.

Work seed st band as follows:

Row 1 (RS): *k1, p1*, rep from * to end of row.

Following rows: k the p sts and p the k sts.

Work 8 more rows in seed st, ending with RS facing for next row.

Next row (RS): k19 (21, 23, 27, 29, 33, 35), work 7 sts seed st in pat as established.

Next row (WS): work 7 sts seed st, p to end of row.

Rep the last 2 rows until piece measures 3" from bottom edge, ending with RS facing for next row.

Joining row: with RS facing, k19 (21, 23, 27, 29, 33, 35), work 7 sts seed st. With RS facing, continue across Center Front hem sts as follows: work 7 sts seed st, k31 (31, 33, 33, 35, 35, 37), work 7 sts seed st. With RS facing, continue across Right Front hem sts as follows: work 7 sts seed st, k to end of row. You should now have all 97 (101, 107, 115, 121, 129, 135) sts on needle. Continue in pat until piece measures 6" from bottom edge, ending with RS facing for next row.

Split for pocket: work first 26 (28, 30, 34, 36, 40, 42) sts for Left Front in pat. Transfer next 45 (45, 47, 47, 49, 49, 51) sts for Center Front to stitch holder and let them hang forward for now. Turn and cast on 45 (45, 47, 47, 49, 49, 51) sts for pocket, adding these

sts to end of first 26 (28, 30, 34, 36, 40, 42) sts. Turn again and work last 26 (28, 30, 34, 36, 40, 42) sts for Right Front. You should now have 97 (101, 107, 115, 121, 129, 135) sts on needle, with Center Front sts hanging forward on holder.

Next row (WS): p19 (21, 23, 27, 29, 33, 35), work 7 sts seed st, p45 (45, 47, 47, 49, 49, 51) for pocket, work 7 sts seed st, p to end.

Next row (RS): k19 (21, 23, 27, 29, 33, 35), work 7 sts seed st, k45 (45, 47, 47, 49, 49, 51), work 7 sts seed st, k to end.

Rep the last 2 rows until piece measures 11" from bottom edge, ending with RS facing for next row. Leave sts on needle for now.

With RS facing, join yarn to Center Front sts on holder.

Row 1 (RS): work 7 sts seed st, k31 (31, 33, 33, 35, 35, 37), work 7 sts seed st.

Row 2 (WS): work 7 sts seed st, p31 (31, 33, 33, 35, 35, 37), work 7 sts seed st. Rep the last 2 rows until length measures 11" from bottom edge, ending with RS facing for next row.

Join top of pocket: work first 26 (28, 30, 34, 36, 40, 42) sts for Left Front in pat. Holding pocket sts behind center front sts, insert right-hand needle into 1st Center Front st and 1st pocket st and k2tog. Continue working in pat in this manner across all Center Front sts and pocket sts to join. Continue in pat across last 26 (28, 30, 34, 36, 40, 42) sts for Right Front. You should now have 97 (101, 107, 115, 121, 129, 135) sts on needle.

Continue working 97 (101, 107, 115, 121, 129, 135) sts for Front in pat until piece measures 20½ (21, 21½, 22, 22, 22, 22)" from bottom edge, ending with RS facing for next row.

Armhole shaping: keeping continuity of pat, bind off 3 sts at beginning of next 4 rows. You should now have 85 (89, 95, 103, 109, 117, 123) sts.

Next row (RS): bind off 2 sts, work 32 (34, 37, 41, 44, 48, 51) sts in pat, p1, *k1, p1*, rep from * 6 more times, work to end of row in pat.

Next row (WS): bind off 2 sts, work 32 (34, 37, 41, 44, 48, 51) sts in pat, work 15 sts seed st, work to end of row in pat.

Keeping continuity of pat as established, complete armhole shaping as follows: bind off 2 sts at beginning of next 4 rows, bind off 1 st at beginning of next 4 rows. Armhole shaping is complete, and you should now have 69 (73, 79, 87, 93, 101, 107) sts.

Split for placket (RS): work 34 (36, 39, 43, 46, 50, 53) sts in pat. Turn, leaving remaining sts on spare needle. Continue working these 34 (36, 39, 43, 46, 50, 53) sts in pat until piece measures 1½ (2, 2¼, 2½, 2¾, 3, 3½)" from beginning of placket opening, ending with RS facing for next row.

Next row (RS): work in pat to last 8 sts, work to end of row in seed st.

Next row (WS): work 8 sts seed st, work in pat to end of row.

Next row (RS): work in pat to last 9 sts, work to end of row in seed st.

Next row (WS): work 9 sts seed st, work in pat to end of row.

Continue in this manner, adding 1 st to width of seed st placket every 2nd row, until seed st placket is 15 (15, 16, 16, 17, 17, 18) sts wide. Work even in pat until length measures (5½ (6, 6½, 7, 7½, 8, 8½)" from beginning of armhole shaping, ending with RS facing for next row. Bind off 19 (21, 23, 27, 29, 33, 35) sts for shoulder; leave remaining 15 (15, 16, 16, 17, 17, 18) sts for collar on a stitch holder.

With RS facing, tie on yarn to first st for right side of placket. Bind off 1 st, work in pat to end of row.

Continue working these 34 (36, 39, 43, 46, 50, 53) sts in pat until piece measures 1½ (2, 2¼, 2½, 2¾, 3, 3½)" from beginning of placket opening, ending with RS facing for next row.

Next row (RS): work 8 sts seed st, work in pat to end of row.

Next row (WS): work in pat to last 8 sts, work 8 sts seed st.

Next row (RS): work 9 sts seed st, work in pat to end of row.

Next row (WS): work in pat to last 9 sts, work 9 sts seed st.

Continue in this manner, adding 1 st to width of seed st placket every 2nd row, until seed st placket is 15 (15, 16, 16, 17, 17, 18) sts wide. Work even in pat until length measures 5½ (6, 6½, 7, 7½, 8, 8½)" from beginning of armhole shaping, ending with WS facing for next

row. Bind off 19 (21, 23, 27, 29, 33, 35) sts purlwise for shoulder; leave remaining 15 (15, 16, 16, 17, 17, 18) sts for collar on a stitch holder.

BACK

Work as for Front up to and including "Joining row."

Work even in pat until piece measures 20½ (21, 21½, 22, 22, 22, 22)" from bottom edge, ending with RS facing for next row.

Armhole shaping: keeping continuity of pat, bind off 3 sts at beginning of next 4 rows, bind off 2 sts at beginning of next 6 rows, bind off 1 st at beginning of next 4 rows. Armhole shaping is complete, and you should now have 69 (73, 79, 87, 93, 101, 107) sts.

Work even in pat until length measures 5½ (6, 6½, 7, 7½, 8, 8½)" from beginning of armhole shaping, ending with RS facing for next row. Bind off all sts.

SLEEVES

Cast on 49 (53, 59, 65, 71, 77, 81) sts.

Work seed st band as follows:

Row 1 (RS): k1, *p1, k1*, rep from * to end of row.

Following rows: k the p sts and p the k sts.

Work 8 more rows in seed st, ending with RS facing for next row.

Proceed in st st; AT THE SAME TIME, when sleeve measures 5" from bottom edge, inc 1 st at each side every 8th row 6 times, to 61 (65, 71, 77, 83, 89, 93) sts. Work even until piece measures 15¾ (16, 16½, 17, 17, 17, 17)" from bottom edge, ending with RS facing for next row.

Sleeve cap shaping: bind off sts at the beginning of each row in the following sequence: bind off 4 sts at each side 1 (1, 2, 2, 2, 3, 3) time(s), bind off 3 sts at each side 1 (2, 2, 2, 2, 2, 3) time(s), bind off 2 sts at each side 2 (2, 2, 3, 3, 2, 3) times, bind off 1 st at each side twice, bind off 2 sts at each side 1 (1, 1, 1, 2, 1, 1) time(s), bind off 3 sts at each side 2 (2, 1, 1, 1, 2, 1) time(s).

Next Row (RS): bind off remaining 19 (17, 21, 23, 25, 25, 25) sts.

FINISHING

Sew shoulder seams.

Collar: with RS facing and using circular needle, work pat across 15 (15, 16, 16, 17, 17, 18) sts on Right Front stitch holder, pick up and knit 31 (31, 33, 33, 35, 35, 37) sts along Back neck edge, work pat across 15 (15, 16, 16, 17, 17, 18) sts on left Front stitch holder. You should now have 61 (61, 65, 65, 69, 69, 73) sts. Continue in seed st until collar measures 2½" from beginning of collar, then bind off in pat (bind off p sts purlwise and k sts knitwise).

Sew side seams and sleeve seams. Matching center of sleeve cap to shoulder seam, and sleeve seam to side seam, sew sleeve to armhole. With WS facing, whipstitch bottom of pocket to inside Front, catching backs of Front stitches so seam is invisible. ❧

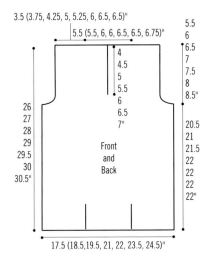

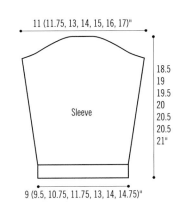

raj

The East Indian genius for color and pattern gets full play in their textiles – in counterpart to the sheer exuberance of their color combinations, they often incorporate symbols with spiritual meaning, such as the lotus motif at the center of this pullover. A tone-on-tone colorway in desert sand shades would be beautiful, too.

SKILL LEVEL: EXPERIENCED

MEASUREMENTS

SIZES (in inches)	TEENS			WOMEN			
	12	14	16	SM	MD	LG	XL
Finished Chest	28½	31	34	37	40½	43	46
Finished Length	18	19	20	21	22	23	23½

MATERIALS

Yarn: Butterfly Super 10 100% Cotton (249 yds or 230 m/125 gr skein). *See also page 126 for yarn information.*

NO. OF SKEINS	TEENS			WOMEN			
	12	14	16	SM	MD	LG	XL
MC: #3459 Peony Pink	3	3	3	4	4	5	5
A: #3553 Canary	1	1	1	1	1	1	1
B: #3402 Nectarine	1	1	1	1	1	1	1
C: #3724 Lime	1	1	1	1	1	1	1
D: #3834 Tile Blue	1	1	1	1	1	1	1

Needles: 1 pr. each U.S. sizes 6 and 7 (4 mm and 4.5 mm) needles OR SIZE TO OBTAIN GAUGE

Spare needle or stitch holder

GAUGE

20 sts and 30 rows = 4" in st st and Fair Isle using larger needles

To work Gauge Swatch: with larger needles, cast on 24 sts and work st st (k all sts on RS and p all sts on WS) until piece measures 3" from bottom edge. Work Chart I, working 8-st rep 3 times across row, reading RS rows of chart from right to left and WS rows from left to right. Carry out-of-work color loosely across WS of work. When Chart I is complete, bind off. Block swatch by laying flat and applying lots of steam with steam iron held just above the swatch. Let cool and dry. If you have too many sts and rows to the inch, switch to a larger needle; too few means you should use a smaller needle. *Hint: you may need to use a larger needle for the Fair Isle sections to achieve consistent gauge and avoid pulling or distorting the knitted garment.*

Your garment will not fit properly if the tension gauge is incorrect! Take the time to check by making gauge swatch.

Directions are given for Teens' size 12. Teens' sizes 14, 16, and Women's sizes Small, Medium, Large, and Extra-Large are given in parentheses. Where there is only one number, it applies to all sizes.

FRONT

With smaller needles and MC, cast on 73 (81, 89, 97, 105, 113, 121) sts.

Work seed st as follows for 4 rows:

Row 1 (RS): k1, *p1, k1*, rep from * to end of row.

Following rows: k the p sts and p the k sts.

Change to larger needles and work Row 1 of Chart I, reading chart from right to left and placing pat as follows: work 8-st rep 9 (10, 11, 12, 13, 14, 15) times across row, then end with St #1. Use Fair Isle method as directed in Gauge Swatch.

Next row (WS): work Row 2 of Chart, reading chart from left to right and placing pat as follows: work St #1, then work 8-st rep 9 (10, 11, 12, 13, 14, 15) times across row.

Charted pat is now in position; work to end of chart, ending with WS facing for next row.

With MC, proceed in st st, beginning with a purl row; AT THE SAME TIME, shape sides: dec 1 st at each side on every RS row 4 (5, 5, 5, 5, 6, 6) times. You should now have 65 (71, 79, 87, 95, 101, 109) sts.

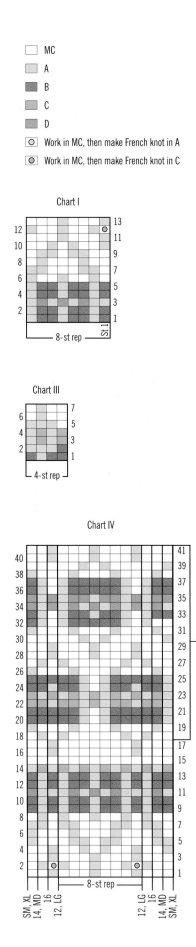

- ☐ MC
- ☐ A
- ☐ B
- ☐ C
- ☐ D
- ◎ Work in MC, then make French knot in A
- ◎ Work in MC, then make French knot in C

Chart I

8-st rep

St 1

Chart III

4-st rep

Chart IV

8-st rep

SM, XL 14, MD 16 12, LG   12, LG 16 14, MD SM, XL

Rep these rows to top of sleeve

Chart II

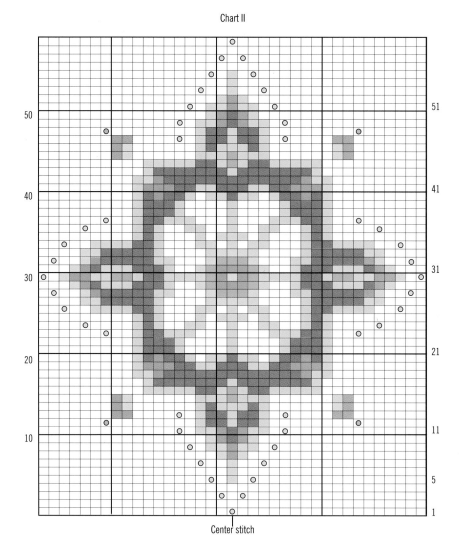

Center stitch

QUICK TIP: *If you need help with any of the patterns in this book, visit the Kirsten Cowan Needleworks website at: **www.kirstencowan.com**.*

Work even, if necessary, until piece measures 4 (4, 4, 4, 4, 4½, 4½)" from bottom edge.

Continue in st st, making 1 inc at each side every 8th row 3 times until you have 71 (77, 85, 93, 101, 107, 115) sts; AT THE SAME TIME, when piece measures 5½ (6, 6, 6½, 7, 7½, 7½)" from bottom edge, begin Chart II on next RS row, establishing placement as follows:

Count the number of sts on needle at this point, subtract 1 from this number and divide by 2. Example: 89 sts - 1 = 88, divided by 2 = 44. With MC, k44 (according to our example); with A work Center st of Row 5 (since Rows 1 through 4 have embroidered sts only); then with MC, k to end of row.

Continue working chart, working A in Fair Isle and using intarsia method for colors B, C, and D (see page 123 for hints on intarsia knitting); AT THE SAME TIME, continue incs at sides as

noted previously until you have 71 (77, 85, 93, 101, 107, 115) sts, then work even until piece measures 10 (10¼, 10½, 10¾, 11¼, 11¾, 11¾)" from bottom edge, ending with RS facing for next row.

Raglan shaping: continuing in st st and Chart II pat as established, bind off 5 (5, 7, 7, 9, 8, 9) sts at beginning of the next 2 rows. You should now have 61 (67, 71, 79, 83, 91, 97) sts.

Next row (RS): k2, sl 1 k1, psso, work in pat to last 4 sts, k2tog, k2.

Next row (WS): p in pat. Rep the last 2 rows 18 (20, 21, 23, 24, 27, 29) more times, to 23 (25, 27, 31, 33, 35, 37) sts, working st st in MC when Chart II is complete. Leave sts on spare needle or stitch holder.

BACK

Work as for Front, but after completion of Chart I, work remainder of Back in plain st st with MC, omitting Chart II.

SLEEVES

With smaller needles and MC, cast on 40 (44, 44, 48, 52, 56, 60) sts.

Work 4 rows seed st as follows:

Row 1 (RS): *k1, p1*, rep from* to end.

Following rows: k the p sts and p the k sts.

With larger needles and B, work 2 rows st st.

Next row (RS): work Row 1 of Chart III, working 4-st rep 10 (11, 11, 12, 13, 14, 15) times across row and using Fair Isle method.

Work to end of chart, ending with WS facing for next row.

With MC, proceed in st st, beginning with a purl row; AT THE SAME TIME, inc 1 at each side on next row, then every following 6th row 7 (7, 10, 10, 11, 11, 12) times. You should now have 56 (60, 66, 70, 76, 80, 86) sts.

Next row (RS): begin Chart IV, placing 8-st rep with additional sts at beginning and end of row as follows: work first 0 (2, 1, 3, 2, 0, 3) sts at right edge of chart, work 8-st rep 7 (7, 8, 8, 9, 10, 10) times, work last 0 (2, 1, 3, 2, 0, 3) sts at left edge of chart. Continue working chart with placement as established. Work to top of chart, then rep Rows 18 through 41 until piece measures 10 (11, 11½, 12, 12½, 13, 13½)" from bottom edge, ending with RS facing for next row.

Raglan shaping: continuing charted pat as established, bind off 5 (5, 7, 7, 9, 8, 9) sts at beginning of the next 2 rows. You should now have 46 (50, 52, 56, 58, 64, 68) sts, ending with RS facing for next row.

Next row (RS): k2, sl 1 k1, psso, work in pat to last 4 sts, k2tog, k2.

Work 3 rows in pat.

Rep the last 4 rows 2 (3, 0, 1, 1, 7, 11) more time(s).

Next row (RS): k2, sl 1 k1, psso, work in pat to last 4 sts, k2tog, k2.

Work 5 rows in pat.

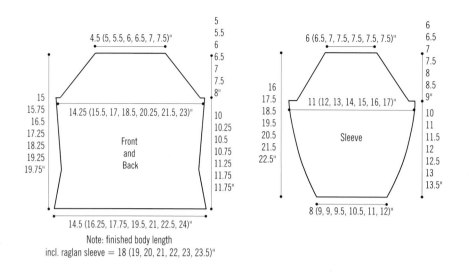

Front and Back diagram:
4.5 (5, 5.5, 6, 6.5, 7, 7.5)"
5 / 5.5 / 6 / 6.5 / 7 / 7.5 / 8"
15 / 15.75 / 16.5 / 17.25 / 18.25 / 19.25 / 19.75"
14.25 (15.5, 17, 18.5, 20.25, 21.5, 23)"
10 / 10.25 / 10.5 / 10.75 / 11.25 / 11.75 / 11.75"
14.5 (16.25, 17.75, 19.5, 21, 22.5, 24)"
Note: finished body length
incl. raglan sleeve = 18 (19, 20, 21, 22, 23, 23.5)"

Sleeve diagram:
6 (6.5, 7, 7.5, 7.5, 7.5, 7.5)"
6 / 6.5 / 7 / 7.5 / 8 / 8.5 / 9"
16 / 17.5 / 18.5 / 19.5 / 20.5 / 21.5 / 22.5"
11 (12, 13, 14, 15, 16, 17)"
10 / 11 / 11.5 / 12 / 12.5 / 13 / 13.5"
8 (9, 9, 9.5, 10.5, 11, 12)"

QUICK TIP: *When working a color motif like the Raj sweater medallion, shown on page 112, you can combine two methods. Since the Canary Yellow color recurs at various points on every row, carry it across the back using the Fair Isle method. For the other colors, use color-blocking, with separate balls of yarn for each area of color.*

Rep the last 6 rows 4 (4, 6, 6, 7, 4, 2) more times, to 30 (32, 36, 38, 38, 38, 38) sts.

Work even in pat, if necessary, until length of raglan seams, measured along edge, matches length of Front raglan seams, ending with RS facing for next row. With MC, bind off.

FINISHING

Embroider French knots as noted on charts (see page 124 for directions on making French knots). Sew raglan seams, leaving left Back raglan seam open.

Neckband: with RS facing, smaller needles, and MC, pick up and knit 26 (28, 32, 34, 34, 34) sts across top of first sleeve, knit across 23 (25, 27, 31, 33, 35, 37) sts from Front stitch holder, pick up and knit 26 (28, 32, 34, 34, 34, 34) sts across top of second sleeve, knit across 23 (25, 27, 31, 33, 35, 37) sts from Back stitch holder for a total of 98 (106, 118, 130, 134, 138, 142) sts.

Next row (WS): *k1, p1*, rep from * to end.

Next row (RS): k2tog, *work seed st, and when you come to corner at raglan seam, work triple dec as follows: insert needle from left to right into next 2 sts at once and slip to right-hand needle, k1, pass 2 slipped sts over last-knitted st*, rep from * to * twice more, work seed st to last 2 sts, k2tog.

Next row (WS): work in seed st.

Next row (RS): with A, bind off knitwise. Sew left back raglan seam and neckband seam. Sew side seams and sleeve seams. ❧

about the patterns

In keeping with my ambition to make knitting patterns easy to read and use, you'll notice a few special features about the instructions in this book. For one, I tend to use fewer abbreviations in my written instructions. Secondly, I like to provide both charted and written instructions where applicable, since I know that both have their devotees. (Please see "Working from Charts," below, if you'd like more information.) Finally, I'd rather be loquacious than laconic in my instructions. For example, instead of writing "Work Left Front as mirror image of Right Front," I'll write out full instructions for both. However, if you have a question or (heaven forbid) you suspect an error in a pattern, please visit www.martingale-pub.com or www.kirstencowan.com to find help.

Some abbreviations are inevitable; for an explanation of the knitting abbreviations and terms used in this book, please see page 120. Diagrams and how-to's for the various stitches and finishing techniques can be found on pages 121 through 124.

WORKING FROM CHARTS

To make a colorwork design, you'll need to follow a chart, and you have the option of using a chart for many of the cabled patterns in this book, too. Our charts are printed in full color rather than the traditional black-and-white symbols, which makes them much easier to use, but do bear in mind that we've focused on making the chart colors easy to distinguish from one another (even on a black-and-white photocopy), so they're not meant to represent the exact shades of the yarns.

To follow a chart, remember that each square represents a single stitch. Starting at the bottom, read each row horizontally. Usually the first row is a RS row; read the RS row from right to left. Then read the next row, which would be a WS row, from left to right. Most often the RS rows are odd-numbered,

with the number at the right edge of the chart where you begin the row, and conversely, the WS rows have even numbers at the left edge of the chart where you begin those rows.

SIZING INFORMATION

Many of the patterns in this book come in seven sizes; usually Small, Medium, Large, and Extra-Large for adults, and 12, 14, and 16 for teens. I know that's a long list of sizes, but writing all of the sizes together, rather than as separate teens' and adults' patterns, allowed me to offer you more designs! To help keep track of your chosen size as you're working through a pattern, use a pencil to lightly circle all of the instructions for your size, before you begin knitting. Or, if the idea of marking up a book is sacrilege, make a photocopy (*for your personal use only, of course*) and highlight the instructions for your chosen size on the copy.

The teen sizes are roughly equivalent to their ages in years, but we all know some 14-year-olds who are taller than their parents while their 16-year-old friends have yet to reach adult size. The smartest solution – and this goes for adults, too – to determine your correct size is to look at a similar sweater that you already own. Measure your sweater across the widest part of the chest, and find the size in the pattern that most closely matches it.

The length of the sweater can usually be adjusted fairly simply: by adding or subtracting inches to the length below the armhole shaping. That's why you shouldn't choose your size based on the pattern's length, but by the chest width. A caveat or two when modifying the length: if you make the sweater longer, remember to purchase extra yarn. And some patterns need to be adjusted by a full pattern repeat, such as a cabled sweater like the Siobhan design on page 33, where you would need to add or subtract the length of a full diamond cable pattern.

A SPECIAL NOTE ABOUT UNISEX PATTERNS AND SLEEVE LENGTHS

Many of the designs in this book that were photographed on a man would look great on a woman, too. To ensure the best fit for a woman's shorter arms and smaller stature, you may have to select a smaller size (see "Sizing Information" on facing page for hints), and you'll need to shorten the sleeve length.

Here's how to figure out how much you need to take off the sleeve length: have someone take your overarm measurement – stand with your back to them and your arm held straight out, and have them measure from the middle of your back neck, across the back of your shoulder, and along your arm to your wrist. Next, look at the schematic drawings that are given with your pattern, showing the finished measurements of each piece. Add half of the neck width, the shoulder width, and the sleeve length for your desired size, to determine the pattern's overarm measurement. For example, if the neck width is 8", the shoulder is 5", and the sleeve length is 23", the finished overarm is 32". If your own overarm measurement is 30", then you need to shorten the sleeves by 2". Using the overarm measurement is much more accurate than simply measuring the sleeve length alone, since that doesn't take into account whether the shoulder is dropped and therefore where the sleeve starts on the arm.

If you do adjust the sleeve length, do so *after* completing the increases at the sides of the sleeve and *before* working the sleeve cap, so that the top of the sleeve will still fit the armhole. If you need help, see the Kirsten Cowan Needleworks web site at www.kirstencowan.com; you'll find answers to most of your questions posted there.

GAUGE SWATCHES

I know you know, but still I feel compelled to remind you: do take a little extra time to check your own gauge by making a gauge swatch. If a sweater design calls for 20 sts to 4", and you knit it too tightly at 22 sts to 4", your sweater will be several inches too small. To avoid this painful result, make the swatch as directed in the pattern, block it, and measure it as shown below. If you obtain more stitches and rows in 4" than the pattern specifies, switch to a larger needle to make your knitting a little looser. And if the opposite is true, you'll need a smaller needle.

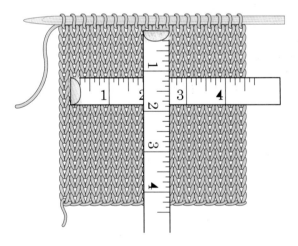

Our gauge swatch instructions are a little unusual in that we ask you to make your swatch with more stitches than you should count; i.e., if the tension should be 18 sts in 4", we'll ask you to make a gauge swatch that's 20 sts wide. That's because the edge stitches can be distorted, so we don't want you to measure right to the edges of your swatch.

terms and abbreviations

bind off
the final row of knitting, prevents unraveling (also called cast off); see Knitting and Finishing Techniques

cast on
begin knitting piece by forming a row of loops on one needle; see Knitting and Finishing Techniques

cn
cable needle

dec
decrease the number of stitches indicated, usually either by k2tog, p2tog, or [sl 1, k1, psso]. See Knitting and Finishing Techniques

garter st
knit all stitches on all rows

inc
increase the number of stitches; see Knitting and Finishing Techniques

k2tog
knit 2 stitches together to form a decrease; see Knitting and Finishing Techniques

k
knit; see Knitting and Finishing Techniques

Left
from the point of view of the person wearing the garment, e.g., the left neck edge is on the wearer's left

M1
a special way to increase the number of stitches; see Knitting and Finishing Techniques

MC
Main Color, or the background color in multicolored garments

mm
millimeter (used for metric needle sizes)

no stitch
used on charts where number of stitches vary on some rows, indicated by a shaded gray square on the chart; skip over these stitches when reading charts

p2tog
purl 2 stitches together to form a decrease; see Knitting and Finishing Techniques

p
purl; see Knitting and Finishing Techniques

pat
pattern

psso
pass slipped stitch over; see Knitting and Finishing Techniques under "sl1, k1, psso"

rep
repeat

Right
from the point of view of the person wearing the garment, e.g., the Right Front is on the wearer's right

RS
Right Side, meaning the side of the piece worn on the outside of the finished garment

sew-through buttons
as opposed to shank button, buttons with holes for sewing to garment

shank buttons
as opposed to sew-through button, buttons with a loop on the back for sewing to garment

sl
slip; meaning slide the next stitch from left-hand needle to right-hand needle without knitting or purling it

st st
stockinette stitch or stocking stitch (knit on right side rows and purl on wrong side rows)

st
stitch

sts
stitches

turn
switch the right-hand needle to your left hand, and vice versa, usually upon completing a row

work even
work straight with no increases or decreases for shaping

WS
Wrong Side, meaning the inside of the piece, worn next to the body on the finished garment

wyib
with yarn in back: the working yarn is held to the back of the piece (the side facing away from you)

wyif
with yarn in front: the working yarn is held to the front of the piece (the side facing toward you)

yo
yarn over; also called yfwd; see Knitting and Finishing Techniques

[...]
indicates a group of stitches, often to be repeated as many times as directed

...
work the directions given between the asterisks, then repeat as many times as directed. When directions say "rep from *," it means you should repeat the directions between the asterisks.

knitting and finishing techniques

The art of knitting is essentially a process of making loops, row upon row.
Starting with a cast-on or foundation row on your left-hand needle, each stitch or loop on
the left-hand needle is transferred to the right-hand needle, while drawing a new loop through it.
When all the stitches have been knitted onto the right-hand needle, one row is complete.
The needles are then switched from one hand to the other, and the next row is begun.
Use the following tips and techniques to make the garments in this book.

THE BASICS

Slip knot

This is worked to make the very first loop on your left-hand needle, to begin casting on. Make a loop, pull a second loop through the first (in the direction shown by the arrow at near right), slip the second loop onto your needle and pull the yarn ends to tighten (as shown at far right).

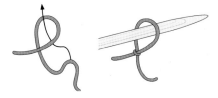

Casting on

Casting on forms a base row or a foundation row needed to start knitting. Begin with a slip knot on your left-hand needle (see above). With the working end of the yarn hanging at the back of the left-hand needle, insert the tip of your right-hand needle from front to back through the front of the loop on the left-hand needle. Wrap the yarn counterclockwise around the tip of the right-hand needle and draw this loop through the original loop on the left-hand needle. So far, you are basically making a knit stitch, but to cast on, you slip that new loop back onto the left-hand needle. You now have two stitches cast on. Keep repeating this sequence to make additional stitches.

The knit stitch

"Knitting" refers to the overall process and also to a specific stitch. Make a knit stitch as follows: With the working yarn hanging at the back of your needles, insert the tip of your right-hand needle from front to back through the loop on the left-hand needle. Wrap the yarn counterclockwise around the tip of the right-hand needle and draw this loop through the original loop on the left-hand needle. Slide the original loop off the left-hand needle, keeping the new loop on your right-hand needle.

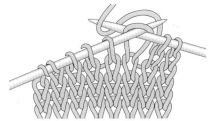

The purl stitch

Purl stitches are often made on the wrong-side rows; when alternated with knit rows, this makes stockinette stitch. With the working yarn hanging at the front of your work, insert the tip of your right-hand needle from right to left through the front of the loop on the left-hand needle, as shown at right. Wrap the yarn counterclockwise around the tip of the right-hand needle as shown, and draw this loop through the original loop on the left-hand needle. Slide the original loop off the left-hand needle, keeping the new loop on your right-hand needle.

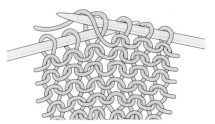

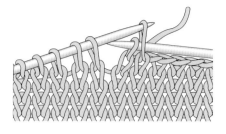

Binding off

To finish off a piece of knitting and keep it from unraveling, you bind off (or "cast off") the top edge. Knit one stitch onto your left-hand needle. *Knit one stitch onto your left-hand needle, then with the point of your right-hand needle, lift the first stitch up and over the last-worked stitch as shown at left, allowing it to drop off the right-hand needle.* Repeat the directions between the asterisks until you have one stitch remaining. Cut the yarn and pull it through this last stitch to fasten.

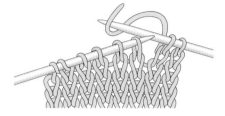

Yarn over

Yarn over (or "yarn forward") forms an increase by wrapping the yarn over the right-hand needle, as shown, before working the next stitch on the left-hand needle. When the yarn over is worked like a normal stitch on the following row, it forms a hole, so it's often used in lace patterns.

SHAPING

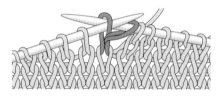

Increase

The traditional increase is made by knitting first into the front of the next stitch, and without drawing it off the left-hand needle, knitting again into the back of the same stitch. Draw both new stitches off the left needle together. You now have two stitches where before you had one.

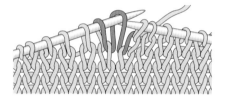

M1

An alternative way of increasing the number of stitches by one stitch: Lift the strand between the next stitch and the last-worked stitch onto your left needle. Knit into the back of this new loop as shown at left.

K2tog decrease

To decrease the number of stitches by one stitch, insert the right-hand needle into the next two stitches at once and knit them together as if they were one. When inserting the right-hand needle, move it from left to right, so that it enters the second stitch, then the first stitch.

P2tog decrease

To decrease the number of stitches by one stitch, insert the right-hand needle into the next two stitches at once and purl them together as if they were one, as shown at left.

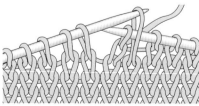

sl1, k1, psso

Creates a decrease of one less stitch, with the decrease slanting to the left. Slip the next stitch to the right-hand needle without knitting it, knit the following stitch as usual, then with the tip of the left-hand needle, lift the slipped stitch up and over the last-worked stitch, allowing it to drop off the right-hand needle.

Fair Isle

A method of knitting using two colors per row, following the color placement on a chart. The color not in use is stranded or floated across the wrong side of the piece, as shown at right. If the float is more than five stitches long, it will pull, so to shorten the float, twist the out-of-work color around the working color approximately every third stitch.

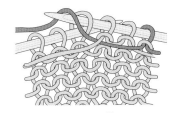

Intarsia

Also known as colorblocking, intarsia is a method of knitting multicolored pieces by using separate balls of yarn for each area of color. *(Hint: for small areas of color, just use one long strand of yarn, which can be untangled by simply pulling it free.)* When you change from one color to another, twist the two colors together on the wrong side of your work to prevent a gap, as shown at right.

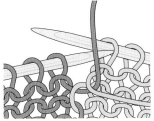

Seams: Vertical edge to vertical edge

For sewing two vertical edges, such as side seams, use the mattress seam shown at right. Worked properly without stretching or distorting the shape of the knitted edges, it's almost invisible and allows just the right amount of stretch.

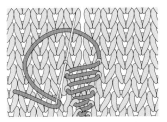

Seams: Horizontal edge to horizontal edge

Where two horizontal edges must be joined, such as at the shoulder seam, use the seam shown at right.

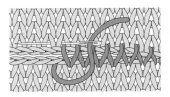

Seams: Horizontal edge to vertical edge

The sewing method shown at right can be used for joining a horizontal edge to a vertical edge, such as a sleeve cap to an armhole.

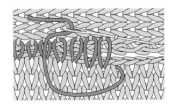

Square armholes

Square armholes have sleeve caps that are straight across – they make for easy knitting while still allowing a good fit at the shoulders. To sew the sleeve cap to the armhole, note that the upper part of the sleeve side seams are sewn to the armhole bound-off stitches, as shown at right.

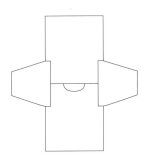

Picking up stitches

Directions for neckbands or button bands often require you to pick up a given number of stitches around the garment edge. Tie on yarn and with right side facing you, insert needle through the full edge stitch (i.e., through two loops), wrap yarn around needle, and draw through the edge stitch. Continue picking up stitches around edge in this manner. Note that you may have to skip edge stitches occasionally, as shown at right. To pick up stitches evenly along a long edge such as the front edge on a cardigan, you may have to measure and divide the edge into halves or fourths, using stitch markers, and divide the stitches accordingly.

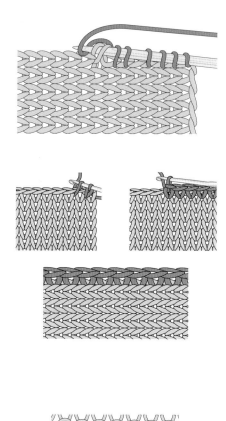

Single crochet edging

With right side facing you, insert the hook through the edge stitch, wrap yarn around hook and pull through edge, forming a loop on hook. Wrap yarn around hook again, and pull through loop on hook. Continue to insert hook through successive edge stitches, first wrapping and pulling the yarn through both the edge stitch and loop on hook, then wrapping again and pulling through new loop on hook. Cut yarn and pull through last loop on hook to finish. This method is worked the same way for either horizontal or vertical edges, both of which are shown at right.

Weaving or darning ends

After you've sewn your garment together, you need to secure the ends of yarn. With wrong side facing, thread the yarn into a tapestry needle and weave it diagonally into the backs of the stitches as shown, then reverse direction and weave into the backs of a few more stitches. This method prevents the ends from pulling loose if the garment is stretched or pulled.

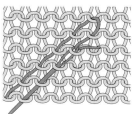

French knots

These are simple decorative embroidery stitches. Thread yarn into a tapestry needle and secure the yarn on the wrong side of the work by weaving in the end (see above), then wrapping it around the back of a stitch a few times. Bring the needle to the right side and wrap yarn around needle counterclockwise as shown at near right. With your left hand, bring yarn around tip of needle as shown at far right, then insert needle into fabric, a halfstitch away from starting point. Draw needle through to wrong side and secure.

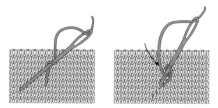

Duplicate stitch

Also known as Swiss darning, duplicate stitch is an embroidery technique that mimics the look of the knit stitch. It's useful for small areas of color – such as the acorn caps on the Autumn design – that are pesky to knit in. Start with your threaded needle on the wrong side, bring it through to the right side at the base of the V that forms the knit stitch. Push your needle through to the wrong side at the top of one side of the V; bring it back to the right side at the top of the other side of the V, and push it to the wrong side at the base of the V.

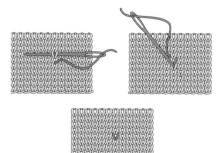

needle conversion chart

U.S. sizes	Metric Sizes*	U.K. sizes
3	3	11
N/A	3.25	10
4	3.5	N/A
5	3.75	9
6	4	8
7	4.5	7
8	5	6
9	5.5	5
10	6	4
10½	6.5	3
N/A	7	2
N/A	7.5	1
11	8	0
13	9	00
15	10	000
17	12.75	N/A
19	16	N/A

*in millimeters

yarn information

One of the great delights of knitting is the sheer tactile pleasure of working with the yarns, from crisp cottons, to lush mohairs, to nubbly alpaca bouclés. In selecting the yarns featured in this book, I gravitated toward natural fibers, for while I think there's a place for synthetic yarns in children's wear, to me they don't provide the same tactile enjoyment in the knitting or the wearing.

Another consideration in selecting yarns was availability. I worked closely with the yarn representatives to find yarns that have wide distribution and were unlikely to be imminently discontinued. Still, we know that it's hard for many of you to find access to good yarns, so we are offering many of the designs in this book in kit form. If you'd like to purchase a kit for one of these designs, please visit the Kirsten Cowan Needleworks website at www.kirstencowan.com to find out more. You may also wish to contact the yarn manufacturer or distributor directly; you'll find their information at right.

ABOUT SUBSTITUTING YARN

If you're interested in using a yarn other than the one specified in my pattern, here's what you need to know. The most popular yarns on the market fall into one of three thickness or weights: Double Knitting (DK), Knitting Worsted (KW), and Chunky-weight. Double knitting yarn is the finest or lightest of the three and is usually knit on U.S. size 6 (4 mm) needles at 22 sts to 4". Next is knitting worsted at 20 sts to 4" width on U.S. size 7 (4.5 mm) needles. Finally, chunky-weight is the heaviest or thickest of the three, at 15 to 18 sts to 4" on U.S. size 9 or 10 (5.5 or 6 mm) needles.

The patterns in this book use these three weights of yarn, with the exception of the Pronto design on page 61. To substitute a yarn, you need to make sure that your replacement yarn is the same weight as the yarn used in the pattern. By way of example, if you use a DK yarn for a pattern written for KW wool, your sweater will be much too tight, since the DK stitches will be smaller in the finer yarn. Check the ball band or the tag of the yarn you want to use; it should give a suggested gauge and needle size, sometimes in the form of a little diagram showing the number of stitches and rows in a 4" square swatch. This tension must match the tension given in the pattern. If in doubt, buy just one ball so you can try a swatch with different sizes of needles.

Theoretically, you could play fast and loose with the yarn weight if you use a big enough or small enough needle – for example, you could knit DK yarn on huge needles to get the tension given for a chunky-weight pattern – but in practice, you'll be disappointed with the results. Use an oversized needle to knit a fine yarn more loosely, and your sweater will droop and stretch out of shape. Use a too-small needle to try to make a heavy yarn fit to a lightweight tension, and you'll have a stiff, unyielding fabric. Stick to yarns in the same weight category as the original yarn specified in the pattern, and your creativity will find just reward.

Once you find a yarn that makes a good substitute, you'll need to calculate how much to buy. Since one wool may yield 100 yards per 50-gram ball and another may yield 85 yards per 50-gram ball, if you simply buy the same number of balls of the latter as specified for the former, you'll run out. Each of the patterns in this book gives a yardage for the suggested yarn; multiply this by the number of balls given for your size to arrive at the total number of yards used. Divide that figure by the number of yards in your substitute yarn to figure out how many balls to buy.
An example: Original yarn = 100 yds per skein. Your size requires 12 skeins, for a total of 1200 yards. Your substitute yarn has 80 yds per skein. Therefore, you'll need to purchase: 1200 yds divided by 80 yds = 15 skeins.

RESOURCES

Note: Though their Canadian addresses are listed here, you may call the following yarn suppliers' 1-800 numbers or visit their web sites to find suppliers in your area.

To find Patons Country Garden DK, Patons Classic Merino Wool:

Patons Yarns
P.O. Box 40
Listowel, ON
Canada N4W 3H3

www.patonsyarns.com

To find Katia Technofur, Schachenmayr Piano, Diamond Cantata, Galway Highland, Indiecita Alpaca:

Diamond Yarn
155 Martin Ross Avenue, Unit 3
Toronto, ON
Canada M3J 2L9
1-800-268-1896
www.diamondyarn.com

or

9697 St-Laurent
Montreal, QC
Canada H3L 2N1

To find Berocco Glacé, Butterfly Super 10, Naturally Café, Naturally Guernsey 10 Ply, Naturally Tibet, Schoeller Esslinger Palma:

S.R. Kertzer Limited
105a Winges Road
Woodbridge, ON
Canada L4L 6C2
1-800-263-2354
www.kertzer.com

To find Young Touch Cotton DK, King Cole Luxury Mohair:

Estelle Designs
2220 Midland Avenue, Unit 65
Scarborough, ON
Canada M1P 3E6
1-800-387-5167

*Many of the designs in this book are available as knitting kits. To purchase a kit consisting of yarn, pattern, buttons, and tote bag, please visit the Kirsten Cowan Needleworks website at **www.kirstencowan.com**.*